The Art of
Church
Canvass

The Art of Church Canvass

Allan J. Weenink, D.D., L.H.D.

Keats Publishing, Inc. New Canaan, Connecticut

DEDICATED WITH GRATITUDE
TO

George L. Fitch and Joseph N. Satjar, Canvass Committee Chairmen par excellence, and Donald A. Wright and James D. Hill, extraordinary associates, and to a superb office staff.

THE ART OF CHURCH CANVASS

ISBN: 0-87983-172-3
Library of Congress Catalog Card Number: 78-69998

Published in 1978 by Keats Publishing, Inc.
36 Grove Street, New Canaan, Connecticut 06840

Printed in the United States of America

CONTENTS

PREFACE

For the most part, this is the story of how a canvass operates in a particular church—a typical church in many respects—yet, a church that for the past ten years has given one dollar to benevolences for every two dollars spent on local mission.

At the same time, this is not an original story. There is much here that may be entirely familiar. Bits and pieces have been gleaned through the years from articles and books, conferences and conversations. A continuing process of refinement has gone into improving the art of canvass, as described in this book. It is not the only way to canvass. But it does describe the cumulative experience of one way to canvass.

Therefore, if this book helps one pastor, one church, one canvass committee to further the mission of Jesus Christ throughout the world by increased commitment, stewardship and tangible support for spiritual ends, then it will have fulfilled its intended purpose.

ALLAN J. WEENINK
First Presbyterian Church
Battle Creek, Michigan

FOREWORD

Stewardship for the Christian involves more than just money. It involves all of life. Of course, the commitment Christians make of their money is a very tangible and important part of the stewardship of their life.

But not all church members respond with the same degree of generosity. Many need to be motivated on a regular basis. Fortunately, many others do respond generously, no matter how negligent the church may be in stimulating a greater consciousness of giving.

In time most congregations generally seek out a financial commitment from their membership deliberately, not only to raise money to meet a budget, but what is more important, to stimulate a great consciousness of the Christian's need to give. The concrete evidence of that giving (and the increase in giving that such stimulation provokes) is the dollars placed in the Sunday morning offering.

Lay and clergy leaders in congregations develop all kinds of procedures for stimulating that response. In most places the process is an on-going, year-long affair culminating in an intensive annual fund-raising effort with personal visits to every member. Variety in approaches to this annual effort abound, but every so often a new technique or concept, proven successful, looms dramatically above all the others previously tried. This book describes one of those more successful plans.

Active congregations are involved in many activities of note and substance. But those with successful programs of membership involvement usually have developed a stewardship program that inspires generous and dedicated giving to the mission of the church. Because giving is good and generous, the programs of that church are more likely to be successful.

At First Presbyterian Church in Battle Creek, Michigan, Pastor Allan J. Weenink has achieved that success. His congregation's program of outreach and service and dedication to mission is evident in many ways, including the stewardship response of its members. And no doubt its total program is successful in part because of the care and planning that go into the details of planning that annual every-member visitation canvass.

This book is the story of how that congregation plans and implements the actual visitation process.

Replete with illustrations of letters and suggestions to detail, this book offers congregational leaders another exceptional resource toward developing a program that challenges greater member giving tactfully, with sensitivity and basic Christian commitment to the mission of the church.

Foreword

This book is not the final answer. It is only one more resource added to hundreds of others already published and yet to come. But here, in *The Art of Canvass*, Pastor Allan J. Weenink has added another valuable aid to that rich collection of stewardship resource materials congregational leaders need and want. The annual visit to members is important. This book tells how those visits can be done creatively, inspirationally, tactfully, successfully.

MANFRED HOLCK, JR.
Publisher-Editor
Church Management: The Clergy Journal

• 1 •

THE ART OF CANVASS

THE-Every-Member Canvass or Visitation can be an exciting and meaningful experience in the life of a local church. It is an instructional vehicle through which something is conveyed to the entire church family and a channel by which people reflect back something of their hopes, aspirations, and concerns. It must always be seen as a two-way street. Certainly the pastor needs to sense the communicative and educative values. This is more than a necessary evil or money raising chore that comes each year as an added administrative burden.

The canvass can challenge the best talents of the creative pastor and the finest resources of the concerned congregation. The pastor has a key role. His or her insights, resourcefulness, enthusiasm, overview and catalytic strengths are part of the contribution that can and must be made to this vital aspect of congregational life.

The canvass in a particular church is really world-wide in scope. Many lives and institutions are influenced by what happens at the local level. Harry Emerson Fosdick made the classic statement: "The avenues are open down which our pennies, our dollars, or our millions can walk together in an accumulating multitude to the succor of all mankind. Each of us can take some of his own nerve and sinew reduced in wages to the form of money, and through money, which is a naturalized citizen of all lands and which speaks all languages, can be at work wherever the sun shines. It is one of the miracles of science that a man busy at his daily tasks at home can yet be preaching the gospel in Alaska, healing the sick in Korea, teaching in the schools of Persia, feeding the hungry in India, and building a new civilization at the headwaters of the Nile." What a perspective that is!

In part, the canvass is an instrument for bringing into harmony the resources that make such a vision possible. It educates, stimulates and motivates. Individuals and congregations are challenged to renewed Christian commitment. Men, women and children as members of the body of Christ are called, express their catholicity and Christianity by putting faith into action. This is no isolated event. The canvass becomes a powerful force in unifying congregational life, extending the mission of a particular church world-wide and deepening the spiritual life of individuals through stewardship.

"A man may decide either to accept or to reject Jesus Christ. But, once he has accepted Christ, it is not for him to decide whether or not he will be a steward, for he becomes a steward when he becomes a Christian. He may be a good steward or he may be a poor steward; nevertheless, he *is* a steward. He has been entrusted with the gospel of Jesus Christ and has been given the gift of eternal life, and it is his high calling to share this gift with others. The one requirement that is placed on a steward is that he be found faithful. The ministry of Christian giving is fulfilled to the extent that a man is faithful in the stewardship of the gospel and of all that is his to share" (Powell, *Money and the Church*, p. 236).

The purpose of the canvass is to motivate the members of the congregation to rethink their stewardship on a regular basis. This is not to be simply a response to a well-presented budget or convincingly-documented needs. The entire enterprise is a means of stimulation, self-examination and spiritual renewal. Its goal: to effect deepened and enlarged Christian stewardship. Therefore, as we talk about the canvass and the budget we are not merely talking about mechanical methods for persuading people to give, or to give more. That may well happen in the process. However, the important thing to keep in mind is that giving is an expression of faith. Paul says, ". . . your very giving proves the reality of your faith" (II Corinthians 9:13—J. B. Phillips). The canvass is a call to witness.

"When a church asks for money, it needs to understand itself as inviting people to participate, as finite creatures and means of finite resources, in that Creativity through which all things are made, and made steadily new. Every believer has the right to experience the joy of genuine self-giving which God experiences in every moment of the universe's existence. The church needs a strategy which will allow such joy to come fully into being. And there is no better place to begin than with the formulation and securing of the annual budget" (Leroy T. Howe, "The Joy of Giving" *Church Management*, November/December 1976). The canvass is an indispensable part of the process of invitation.

Music, painting, drama and dance are considered forms of art. In their highest meaning, they are expressive ways of glorifying God. The canvass, too, is an art. It harmonizes practical components and lofty ends, creatively, to the glory of God.

• 2 •

THE CANVASS CALENDAR

A SUCCESSFUL canvass involves details and timing as well as creativity. Weeks of planning and activity precede the actual event. One of the first steps is the preparation of pledge cards, beginning in late summer. The name of the member/members of each pledging unit is typed in the upper left hand corner of the card and the amount of the current pledge is typed in the appropriate space (note the chapter on the Pledge Card). This work should be completed before October 1.

The minister and the canvass committee chairperson meet together in late summer or early fall to organize and plan for the ensuing weeks. An initial item is calculating the number of callers needed. This can be done by counting the family units in the congregation. Plan for each visitor to make approximately five calls. Take into consideration that no call is made at the home of visitors. Ascertain the number of homes where no visit will be made because of special circumstances. Families living out of town should also be subtracted from the total. They will be contacted by letter. Then, determine how many callers are essential for the visitation. Add at least twenty percent to the total. Many of those asked will be unable to serve for various reasons.

The minister and chairperson then select the names of those to be invited. This can be done by going through the church rolls. Give thoughtful consideration to each individual. These people have an important function. They are representatives of the church. Interpretation and listening is involved. Some are more qualified for this role than others. Careful selection of callers is a key factor.

Type an alphabetical list of these names including address and telephone number. Keep a wide right hand margin. Make three columns at the right side of the sheet: "can call November 1," "can follow-up November 15," "comments." This master record will eventually have a "yes" or "no" opposite each name. When "no" a comment such as "out of town," "going into hospital," "does not care to be a visitor," should be noted. Eventually it tells the number of people available to serve and is used to prepare mailings for these individuals. Save it for the next year as a reference when selecting canvassers.

A calendar should be developed detailing the various mailings and the necessary office preparation. The following outline will be expanded in succeeding chapters.

The Canvass Calendar

CANVASS MAILINGS AND MATERIAL
(based on a calendar year when November 1 is a Sunday)

1. *October 12* Address one set of white and one set of colored 3 x 5 cards for all member units (e.g.—Mr. and Mrs. John Q. Smith or Miss Joan S. Jones or Mr. Robert D. Johnson). If the church has geographical zones or a parish plan, the zone number should be placed in upper right hand corner.

2. *October 12* Address packets (envelopes 5¾ x 8¾) for all members.

3. *October 19* Retired people, canvass committee, or youth—sort, collate and stuff various mailings.

4. *October 19* Letter concerning Youth Budget for all church school teachers and officers.

5. *October 20* Letter to out-of-town members inviting them to make a pledge on Loyalty Sunday. Pledge card and copy of budget included.

6. *October 23* Packets to canvassers with: letter, copy of budget, inspirational insert and pledge card. The letter indicates this is the same packet they will deliver on Visitation Sunday and gives additional details about that day.

7. *October 23* Packets to those unable to canvass with letter, copy of budget and pledge card.
   October 23 Letter to college students with budget and pledge card.

8. *October 24* Youth Budget information to parents of all church school children—three years through senior high.

9. *October 27* Letter to entire congregation (except out of town members) with information about Visitation Sunday, Loyalty Sunday and inspirational insert.

10. *October 28* List all "yes" callers alphabetically—name only.
    October 28 Type three copies of call sheets (half sheets) with grouped calls, using the pre-arranged white cards which have been organized by canvass committee.

15

11. *October 29* Special letter to those who will not be called on: sensitive individuals, people in nursing homes and hospitals, etc.

12. *October 30* Letter to young adults.

13. *October 31* Second letter to church school parents with children age three through sixth grade. Letter contains pledge card for each child in family under grade six and mimeographed inspirational insert.

14. *October 31* Letter to youth, grades seven through twelve. Letter contains pledge card and inspirational insert.

15. *November 4* Letter to non-members who are related to church by regular attendance, children in church school, youth groups or through other involvement. Letter contains pledge card and church budget.

16. *November 4* Letter to drivers for youth canvass on November 8.

17. *November 4* Letter to those not home on Sunday, November 1. Packets not delivered on Visitation Sunday are returned to church and mailed with cover letter.

18. *November 5* Letter of thanks to canvassers.

19. *November 11* Letter of reminder to follow-up callers.

20. *November 11* Letter to members who have not returned pledges on Loyalty Sunday indicating a visit if pledge is not received by Sunday, November 15.

21. *November 12* Follow-up letter to out-of-town members who have not pledged.

22. *November 17* Follow-up letter to youth in grades seven through twelve who have not pledged.

23. *December 3* Letter to those who have not returned pledges indicating present pledge will carry over into the new year.

24. *December 28* Letter with final request for pledge to those who have contributed currently but have not pledged for new year.

25. *December 28* Letter to those who have not given during current year and have not pledged for new year.

Develop an order sheet by late summer indicating the material necessary for various mailings and quantity. Denominationally prepared stewardship items should be reviewed. There are other creative sources for helpful and effective brochures, flyers, posters and inserts such as Louis Neibauer Co. of Ivyland, Pennsylvania. Decide what material to purchase and order it to arrive by early October. The prepared mailing schedule can detail the amount and type of material necessary for a particular mailing. Figures and notes can be listed in the margin. When order arrives, these notes refresh the memory.

Special letterheads, bulletins, budget brochures, mailing envelopes, and packets (5¾ x 8¾ inches) may be purchased from denominational sources, stewardship specialists such as the Neibauer Co., or designed and prepared locally. A member of the congregation experienced in public relations or printing and layout can be most helpful in preparing thematic material specifically for the local canvass. This can vary in color, stock and art work so a fresh approach is generated annually. Many churches design and write all their own material which can be printed or produced on various types of duplicating machines. All supplies should be available sufficiently ahead of time for addressing and other handling.

• 3 •

THE CANVASS COMMITTEE

THE minister and canvass chairperson along with at least five carefully selected people are the core group in motivating, organizing and following through on the entire operation. These people function together year after year as an increasingly efficient team, familiar with every aspect of the canvass. They keep things on target.

Usually a canvass committee is selected at the beginning of the year, along with other church committees. The full group includes the chairperson, core committee and sufficient people to serve as recruiters and follow-up personnel. Recruiters should be chosen for their ability to enlist others to serve. They should be veteran visitors who will later act as follow-up callers and substitutes on Visitation Sunday.

The initial meeting for recruiters ought to be held by the first Sunday of October. Notification is sent by the chairperson at least ten days in advance. The minister presides and discusses the meaning and importance of the project. Suggestions are shared, and the budget reviewed. Since these people will follow up, there is op-

18

portunity to discuss that role. They do not canvass on Visitation Sunday but are reminded to be present that day as replacement callers. Their particular task is to recruit ten or twelve fellow members to call on Visitation Sunday. Techniques of telephone invitation are covered as they prepare to enlist others. A mimeographed information sheet is distributed with appropriate comments.

Information and Instructions for Canvass Committee
in Seeking Visitors for Visitation Sunday

1. The people on your list have not received any previous request for their services this year.
2. When you telephone, be positive and expect a positive answer.
3. We expect to enlist the services of at least ___ people to work on this visitation.
4. Visitation Sunday is November 1.
5. The visitors will:
   a. Be guests of the church for dinner on November 1, at 12:30 p.m. in Fellowship Hall.
   b. Make 4 to 6 calls that afternoon.
   c. The call is to consist of delivering a packet and telling the story of First Church's program.
   d. The visitor is NOT to ask for the pledge.
   e. Training instructions will be given at dinner on November 1.
   f. Visitors will call singly.
6. Secure a definite "yes" or "no" answer.
7. All officers, unless out of town or ill, are expected to be callers.
8. Those who cannot visit on November 1 may be enlisted to drive for the Youth Budget Canvass on November 8, or to follow up on November 15.

9. Don't call names circled in ink. They are canvass committee members and have already been enlisted.

10. By Friday, October 15, all workers are to be committed and names called to the church office. When calling names to office, please indicate reason for a "no" response (out of town, not interested in visiting, etc.).

11. Your packet will be mailed on October 23. You will get the same letter as a "yes" visitor. Remember: you do not canvass on the first of November but serve on a standby basis. You will follow-up on November 15. A letter of reminder will be mailed previous to that date.

12. Thanks for your help. Report back promptly.

During the discussion, the canvass chairperson divides the names to be called by the number of people present. This gives the total to be contacted by each recruiter. The chairperson then takes a carbon copy of the record listing all potential callers. The recruiter's name is written on the carbon and also on the left margin of the original copy, opposite the names assigned to that particular person. When calling the office, the secretary quickly finds the name and assigned calls. The recruiter then reads the list: "John Smith is a yes," "Mary Jones is a no, but will follow up on the 15th; she will be out of town on November 1." This is all recorded on the right hand margin in the three columns reading: "November 1," "November 8" and "Comments." An answer is required for every name on the list. Sunday night is suggested as an ideal time for securing visitors. Many recruiters leave the meeting and within an hour have all their people contacted.

The core committee persons are a specialized

group with a number of vital tasks to perform. They organize the calls by geographical zones, determine the number of visits for each canvasser, assemble all material in preparation for Visitation Sunday and audit the pledge cards on Loyalty Sunday. This involves two to five evenings, the Saturday before November 1, Visitation Sunday and Loyalty Sunday. Without them the canvass does not function. These must be highly competent, thoroughly dependable and utterly trustworthy individuals. Since they tabulate all pledges on Loyalty Sunday, discretion is demanded. The canvass chairperson deploys them as personal assistants during the entire project.

In some churches the full canvass committee is also used to prepare mailings and correlate materials. This can usually be done in one or two evenings. Many congregations use retired people for special office projects. These people are eager for useful service. Their help is invaluable at canvass time. On the day assigned, usually in mid-October, a noon luncheon is served the senior citizen work force. A canvass committee person or staff member serves as coordinator. They are divided into several units each with a specialized task. Much work is accomplished in a short amount of time and all key mailings are ready to be sent. This takes a considerable load from the office which has already duplicated the various materials and addressed all envelopes. When completed, the individual mailings are placed in separate boxes. Tape an identifying letter on the box or mark it by number. The mailing coordinator is responsible for getting each set of letters out on the correct date. Everything is now completed well ahead of schedule. This allows the office adequate time for normal functions while avoiding last minute pressures.

• 4 •

GETTING THE CANVASS
VISITS ORGANIZED

AN ESSENTIAL step in organizing the canvass is the preparation of two sets of 3 x 5 cards (one white and one colored), with the name and address of all local residents. This should be done by giving units: Mr. and Mrs. John Q. Smith, 111 Capital Ave., City. Make a separate card if there is a young adult, maiden lady or brother by the same name at the same address. So, in addition to Mr. and Mrs. John Q. Smith, we may also have William R. Smith (young adult, unmarried and living at home), Franklin S. Smith (widower, brother of John, living at the same address), and Miss Mary A. Young (maiden sister of Mrs. Smith, living at the same address). The cards are initially prepared in alphabetical order. Place the parish zone number in the upper right hand corner of each card. Complete by the second week in October.

In addition to the above, other specialized lists should be organized.

1. All members living beyond visitation range of the church. They will receive a personal letter instead of a call.
2. Those in rest homes, hospitals, or situations where it would be unwise to send a visitor.

23

3. Those who have expressed negative thoughts about being visited or have a mental block about a stewardship call. This list will grow through the years as callers report back reactions. Do not make unwanted calls. Send a special mailing. These people usually have no problem with pledging, only the canvass visit.
4. Those members of substantial means or standing in the community who should have a peer call.
5. Those at college locally or away at school. They will receive a special college communication.
6. A list of canvass committee people and potential callers has already been completed.

At least two weeks before the visitation, members of the core group gather to place the white 3 x 5 cards in call groupings. First of all those people named on lists 1 to 6 are removed and the respective cards set aside for later handling. The core committee then goes to work roughing out the calls, beginning with five or six stops per visitor. This can vary. Distance or difficulty in finding an isolated location may suggest a smaller assignment. On the other hand, when many people live in apartments adjoining the church, seven or eight visits are possible. Cumulative experience eventually produces balanced work loads.

Use a large city or county map for estimating distances and locating unfamiliar streets. When cards are grouped in sets of calls, paper-clip together and place in a 3 x 5 file drawer by parish zones. Later, the canvass chairperson will want to double-check them. If for some reason a card needs to be pulled, the chairperson first notes the alphabetical file (colored cards) for zone and then goes to that category for the particular name.

Getting the Canvass Visits Organized

On the Thursday before Visitation Sunday, calling lists are typed on half-sheets (8½ x 5½) from the cards grouped by zones. The half-sheet contains the names and addresses of those people assigned to one particular caller. Names correspond to the number of 3 x 5 cards clipped together in a set. Make three copies.

On Friday evening before the canvass, the core committee meets in Fellowship Hall or wherever the Sunday meal will be served. Some churches are blessed with a stage. This is an ideal place to set up extra tables for arranging the calls. Or use a room adjoining the dining hall. The committee lays out the half-sheets (caller lists in triplicate) so that every set of calls is placed flat. The matching set of 3 x 5 cards is laid on top of the call sheets.

The minister, a staff person or the canvass chairperson then assigns a visitor to a particular set of calls. Each set has been numbered chronologically. The assignment person, who is thoroughly familiar with the congregation, has in hand a list of all canvassers. Viewing a specific set of people to be visited, an immediate mental picture forms of the appropriate person for that group. The assigner consults the list of callers and, finding that "right" person, writes the number of the half-sheet opposite that person's name. The name of the caller is then placed on all three half-sheets. Eventually every name on the assignment sheet will have a number and every set of sheets will have the name of a caller.

This particular process is important. A successful canvass depends on how well it is done.

Usually the pastor can be very effective here. He or she is familiar enough with the congregation to be able to form an instant picture of every group of names. One set may be predominantly retired people, all very gracious and loyal to the church. A neophyte caller could be given this particular group. The new and nervous visitor receives assurance from these saints of the church, and the task is not nearly as awesome as anticipated. They in turn are delighted to see young leaders of the church getting involved. It is a happy matching of calls and caller. On the other hand, there may be mostly dynamic young executives in another set. It is imperative that someone who can match their strengths be sent to visit. Prominent citizens should contact their peers. The art of assignment is a key factor. Although this kind of selectivity is time-consuming, it brings a unique harmony and pays enormous dividends.

After each group has been assigned a caller, the core committee places a packet on the half-sheet for every name. When completed, each pile has: three call sheets with the same number in the upper right hand corner; the name of the person making those particular calls; a 3 x 5 card for every call on the list; a packet addressed to each person on the list; and a piece or pieces of denominational literature for each visit to be made.

Next, separate every eight sets of calls (to correspond with seating capacity of dining room tables) and identify with a number. This insures quick and efficient distribution following the meal and training session on Sunday. At that time, core committee members go directly to their assigned tables with the proper material. All sets are marked with the name of a person sitting at that table. The whole distribution is accurate and takes but a few minutes.

One person makes name tags for each caller. The upper-right-hand corner is numbered, designating table seating. Name tags are placed at the dining room entrance. When callers arrive on Sunday after service, they immediately pick up their name tag with table assignment on it. Each table has a large identifying number so that visitors go promptly to their places.

As soon as the Sunday meal begins the canvass chairperson checks name tags. If there are any left, it means someone with a designated list is not present. An immediate telephone call is made to that person's home. Some crisis may have developed, preventing participation. This means that a recruiter, present on a standby basis, is given an assignment. Committee people eat at a separate table. The chairperson can quickly select a person to cover for the missing visitor. An experienced caller is on hand to substitute. A change is promptly made. Every home will be visited as planned and projected to the congregation.

There are other details to be covered during the dining hour. The core committee people remove the two carbon half-sheets, after any and all changes have been made. One set is to be used as a check list when the visitors report back. The other can serve a later purpose. Our church regularly uses these call sheets for World Wide Communion contact the following September. The caller who visited a certain group of homes on canvass is asked to invite these same people to World Wide Communion. It works beautifully. In September the church office places a telephone number opposite each name on the list. Those who have moved or died are crossed off. The sheet is sent to the person whose name appears in the upper right hand corner. It is accompanied by a letter from the pastor:

Dear Friend:

Each year we contact every member of the church reminding them of World Wide Communion. The response has always been most favorable, resulting in a large congregation for that important day.

Therefore, I would like to ask you to assist in this program of personal contact. Enclosed are the names of those you called on during the Every-Member-Visitation last November. Would you telephone these same people and invite them to be present for World Wide Communion on Sunday, October 1?

A simple, neighborly, gracious call can be very meaningful. It helps to maintain our total church family relationship and intimacy. If, in your conversations, you find those who are ill or in need of pastoral care, please call the church office. Thanking you in advance for this service to your church,

I remain,

Faithfully,
Your Pastor

Getting the Canvass Visits Organized

One small sheet is put at each plate on Visitation Sunday, covering some of the routine details of reporting back. This is given verbally during the training session following Sunday dinner. However, it is good for the callers to have in hand when discussing it and to carry with them as a reminder.

VISITATION SUNDAY, NOVEMBER 1

ALL CALLS MUST BE COMPLETED BY 8:30 p.m., MONDAY, NOVEMBER 2. Those not completed should be turned in that evening. *DO NOT* leave packet when no one is at home. Return packet to the church and it will be mailed with a cover letter. However, *DO* leave a copy of the denominational brochure with a note on the front cover inviting people to church on Loyalty Sunday, November 8. Sign your name. Leave brochure in door or some other obvious place.

TURN IN ALL WHITE CARDS, COMPLETED OR UNCOMPLETED. JOT DOWN ANY USEFUL AND HELPFUL INFORMATION. ALSO, PLEASE RETURN HALF-SHEETS WITH YOUR LIST OF CALLS. REPORT BACK TODAY ON THOSE CALLS COMPLETED.

Refreshments will be served in the later afternoon, November 1, for all callers.

NOVEMBER 15

We will need additional people to assist the canvass committee in making follow-up calls on those who have not pledged by the 15th. There will be a brief meeting at 3:30 p.m. in the Parlor on that day. Those making follow-up calls will have one week to complete the three to five names assigned. Volunteers please write: "Yes—15th" on name tag and leave on table.

· 5 ·

THE PLEDGE CARD

The pledge card is an important tool in the canvass. Most denominations prepare a general basic card which can be obtained free or at a nominal cost. However, there is a great value in having the card printed locally, designed and worded to complement the annual canvass theme. The date and some lines are changed each year. Wording needs to stress gratitude and responsibility along with proportionate giving. Also, recognize the unforeseen by indicating that the pledge can be altered at any time.

Head the card with an attention-getting phrase which will later be included on stationery and other material. Since the pledge card is the first item printed, the theme for the canvass must be determined by early summer. The following are phrases which can set the tone of the canvass: "To the Glory of God," "From Challenge to Achievement," "Stepping Up for Spiritual Service," "To Maintain and Enlarge," "Our Call to Responsible Involvement," "From Strength to Strength," "We Have One Increasing Purpose," "You Are There," "Count Me, Therefore, a Part-

31

ner," "Love Never Ends—It Grows," and "In Joyful Response."

The size of the card can vary. However, a 3 x 5 card seems most practical for filing and handling. All samples shown can be printed on a 3 x 5 card.

TO THE GLORY OF GOD

In gratitude to God and in loyalty to Christ, I accept my responsibility as a Christian. Therefore, I desire to give a fair proportion of my income on a regular basis, for the work of Christ's Church at home and abroad. I wish to subscribe the following amount to enable First Church to carry on its increasing operating, benevolence and improvement programs for the year 19__. I understand that this pledge may be altered, due to the unforeseen, by calling the Financial Secretary.

For Local Mission
(The program of First Church)

19__
WEEKLY

For General Mission   PRESENT   PLEDGE
(Our concern for others)   PLEDGE $ . . . .
                                   PER WEEK
For Capital Funds $ . . . .
(Debt payment and major
   improvements)

. . . .   Name . . . .
      Date   Address . . . .

During the summer, the financial secretary types the family name in the upper left hand corner of the card: Mr. and Mrs. Donald Q. Jones," or "Miss Wilma J. Smith." Then, the amount of the current pledge is typed in the appropriate space. Note that the space for the new pledge is slightly elevated above the present pledge. This stimulates thinking toward an increase or "stepping up" the amount. Later we will discuss the long range program of stepping-up each year.

The next sample is very specific about suggesting an increase. The amount of the pledge for the current year is listed. This is essential for comparative purposes. People need to visualize what they are giving as they consider an increase, or in some cases, a decrease. The next column says, "to be increased." In the far right column is a place for the new pledge. Before a person writes an amount for the coming year he or she must cross the middle column, "to be increased." This is a highly suggestive approach. Some congregations might feel too pressured by this form. It could also be argued that this is the kind of stimulating and positive approach necessary in pointing people to sacrificial stewardship. A conscientious person with limited circumstances might be troubled going from the first column to the third without some kind of increase. The middle column could exercise an undue pressure so that people responded more from stimulus than genuine commitment. Yet, there are many who need to be strongly motivated. Unquestionably the middle column makes one think. The stewardship committee will want to weigh the relative merits and possible problems. For some congregations it has been a successful method of stimulating increases.

COUNT ME, THEREFORE, A PARTNER

In gratitude to God and in loyalty to Christ, I accept my responsibility as a Christian. I therefore subscribe the following amount to enable First Church to carry on its increasing operating and benevolence programs for the year 19__.

	Present Pledge Per Week	To Be Added Per Week	Total 19__ Weekly Pledge
For Local Mission	$	$	$ . . . .
For General Mission			

. . . .
Date

Name ....
Address ....

Another type of card has only one space for listing a new pledge. This can be used with non-members, placed in pew racks on Loyalty Sunday for those who forget the original card, sent in follow-up letters, carried by follow-up visitors, and mailed to new members who join the church during the year.

The Pledge Card
TO THE GLORY OF GOD

In gratitude to God and in loyalty to Christ . . .
(use the paragraph shown on first card).

For Local Mission
(The on-going program of First Church)   MY TOTAL
                                              PLEDGE
For General Mission
(Our concern for the needs of others)

                                              $ . . . . . .
For Capital Funds
(Mortgage payments and improvements)

. . . .   Name ....
   Date
                          Address ....

Following the Loyalty Sunday service, pledge
cards are brought to the church office where the
financial secretary and core committee members
handle them. As stated above, the core committee remains intact from year to year (except,
of course, to be replaced should a member move,
die or resign). They become an efficient team
handling all details with professional dispatch.
Curiosity about pledges is not a factor. They re-
tain a competent objectivity after working with
the cards year after year.

First, the cards need to be alphabetized. Then,
in a designated place on the right margin, the
workers translate the pledge into a yearly total.
This can be done with the aid of charts which
give the total of a $4.75 per week or $6.35 per
week pledge over a period of fifty-two weeks.
Some banks furnish such charts or a committee
person can prepare several in advance. When
this is finished a complete yearly total can be

quickly tabulated for comparison with the amount pledged on Loyalty Sunday of the previous year.

The core committee can also gather other data for later use by recording the number of pledge increases or decreases. This will leave a balance figure indicating no change. As part of the comprehensive giving pattern it is important to know what yearly changes occur. Officers can later interpret such figures and use the information with the congregation. When this has been completed the pledges are placed in a metal 3 x 5 file drawer for ready reference. Should someone decide to alter a pledge during the year, the new amount is noted on the pledge card and financial statement.

The core committee can also use the cards to record the number of pledges by dollar categories. The following table shows one way of presenting the material. It can be published in the church newsletter or bulletin. This visual form is helpful in discussions with church officers or committees by documenting trends. Individuals also ought to be aware of their standing in the total church-giving profile.

The Pledge Card
FIRST CHURCH OF BLANK CITY
FIVE YEAR ADULT PLEDGE ANALYSIS

	1972	1973	1974	1975	1976
Less than $1.00 per week	33	33	30	27	21
$2.00 per week and over	83	76	61	57	62
$3.00 per week and over	55	49	48	43	46
$4.00 per week and over	34	35	36	31	29
$5.00 per week and over	22	17	16	17	19
$6.00 per week and over	14	14	15	16	14
$7.00 per week and over	18	14	8	8	12
$8.00 per week and over	8	9	12	10	11
$9.00 per week and over	4	6	3	3	3
$10.00 per week and over	12	12	15	12	15
$11.00 to $14.00 & over	14	15	17	18	19
$15.00 to $19.00 & over	7	9	11	17	16
$20.00 to $24.00 & over	4	3	5	5	7
$25.00 to $30.00 & over	3	4	4	5	6
$31.00 to $39.00 & over	0	0	1	2	4
$40.00 to $49.00 & over	1	0	2	2	5
$50.00 to $70.00	1	1	2	2	3
	349	330	319	308	314

1975 Pledge increases	129
1975 Pledge decreases	13
1975 No change	166
1976 Pledge increases	132
1976 Pledge decreases	11
1976 No change	171

	1972	1973	1974	1975	1976
Per Capita Giving—First Church	$122.	$131.	$160.	$161.	$163.
Per Capita Giving for denomination	$127.	$145.	$162.	$178.	$182.

Members making no pledge	91 (1976)	90 (1975)	89 (1974)
Non members making pledge	10 (1976)	5 (1975)	4 (1974)

• 6 •

VISITATION SUNDAY

FOLLOWING the church service on November 1, all visitors report to the dining room and pick up their name tag with table assignment on it. A member of the core committee serves as greeter and interprets seating arrangements. By not offering a seating option people are placed with others they may have never met before. Acquaintances are broadened. Good fellowship is enjoyed. A spirit of anticipation prevails. An ideal atmosphere is established in which to launch the enterprise.

Immediately following the meal the minister welcomes all callers. Here is an appropriate place for humor, adding to the relaxed and expectant atmosphere. This can be followed by a film or filmstrip giving techniques of visiting or an overview of mission. A local church can develop its own helpful interpretation program. Each year an audiovisual committee photographs every activity of the congregation. These are made into slides. Varying insights are projected by changing the theme annually. The initial presentation is made at the Congregational

Meeting to show members the scope of their ministry. Such visibility helps individuals identify with everything their church is doing. Someone can read a prepared script or tape the narrative. This same set of slides may be shown again following the meal on Visitation Sunday. New insights are generated in preparation for the calls to be made. Incidentally, such a presentation is also ideal for new member orientation.

Another interpretive device is the flip chart. A selected member of the campaign committee might use this effective instrument in documenting budget increases. Other methods of stimulating interest, generating enthusiasm and providing factual information will emerge to meet the specific needs of a particular congregation. Forms of drama and musical interpretation adapted for this occasion have proven very effective. Techniques and approaches should change from year to year. Use different members of the congregation with special talents who will motivate the visitors. This adds depth and sparkle to the message they will bring to the homes of the people.

The pastor has a unique role in challenging these callers. Each year vary the emphasis so that those who call regularly will become increasingly knowledgeable about the full ministry and mission of their congregation. All interpretation should be strengthened with a sound theology of stewardship. Occasionally, callers need to be conditioned for questions on difficult and even unpopular denominational actions vexing the flock. Thoughtful pastors realize that newsletter articles and sermons from the pulpit will not answer all questions of the man in the pew, particularly on sensitive issues. This is where the canvass can be helpful. Fruitful discussion concerning needs and problems takes place when lay people communicate during the every-member-visitation.

Sensitive pastors understand that members are often less than candid with the clergy. Therefore, trained lay people must be trusted to handle issues that may only surface in the privacy of a parishioner's living room. At that point, the parishioner is on home turf. Feelings can run the gamut from anger to indifference. The canvass allows the person in the pew to react as an individual. Canvassers offer a sympathetic ear and winsome witness. Such therapy is invaluable for congregational health.

The minister ought to emphasize four specific things in the training talk. These basics are initial conversation points for the visitor.

First, thank your fellow members for their support of the church. Every year by the grace of God and the faithfulness of the congregation, we have managed—some years better than others—but we've managed. We are grateful and want to thank our fellow members for their loyalty. *Therefore, give thanks.*

Second, participate in dialogue—inviting people to express their concerns and offer their constructive criticism. Remind them that their suggestions are put into practice. People need to verbalize. Some talk about things they don't like.

Others speak of things they appreciate. Communication is a two-way street. You will have an opportunity to hear the cares, concerns and feelings of the people. Some questions you can answer from your own experience or knowledge. However, if you can't give an answer, assure them someone will provide the information in the next few days. Each visitor can witness in a personal way. A genuine Christian sharing can be a significant experience for you and those being visited. No rehearsed speech is necessary. Simply say what you sincerely feel as the opportunity is available. *Share.*

Third, participate in evangelism. Invite those you visit to attend church on Loyalty Sunday and bring their pledge for dedication. Some may indicate they will be there as usual. Others will say they haven't been to church for some time. Many will make excuses. This is the place to encourage faithful attendance. Some may have reasons, real or imaginary, for not being present. Give loving encouragement to those who have become careless in their worship responsibilities. Reason with those who have rancor in their hearts. Blessed healing can take effect during such a conversation. Welcome the delinquent to return and the wanderer to renewed interest. *Invite.*

Fourth, talk stewardship. When leaving the packet say something about stewardship. That is the essential purpose of the contact. Indicate that the budget is being increased and, hopefully, every member will respond in kind. It is the time to talk about taking that step up, whether it be a half percent or whatever percentage—not an amount—a percentage. *Challenge to steward-ship.*

Next, the canvass chairperson talks about calling procedure:

1. Relax. Have a pleasant afternoon. These are friendly visits. You'll find this a rewarding experience. Don't just leave the packet with a few terse remarks. Stay awhile and tell the people what your church means to you.
2. Mention the budget increase. This is a sign of progress. A church that does not increase its budget year after year is standing still or going backwards.
3. Invite the people to read the material in the packet carefully.
4. Urge them to be in church on Loyalty Sunday when we dedicate ourselves anew and ask God's blessing on what we pledge.
5. Graciously discuss questions or concerns that might be raised.
6. Indicate that pledges may be changed or cancelled at any time, due to the unforeseen, by calling the office. No questions are asked. A pledge may also be increased at any time.
7. Remind the people to pray about their pledge, review their giving, and increase if possible.

Procedure—

1. Make sure you have a packet for each 3 x 5 card, a half-sheet listing your calls and denominational material to leave at each home.
2. Record your reaction to the visit on the 3 x 5 card. We will follow up on all suggested calls.
3. High School youth give through the Youth Budget. They have their own canvass.

Material for college-age youth has already been mailed.

4. Report back today on all calls. Return your half-sheet and the 3 x 5 cards with comments.

5. Double back on calls where no one is at home. Some may be out to dinner, returning at a later time.

6. Please call between 2:00 p.m. and 5:00 p.m. The congregation has been notified to expect you between those hours.

7. Do not leave the packet when people are not home. Write a note of invitation on the denominational brochure. Return the packet to the church for mailing. It contains the pledge card with privileged information.

8. Small community maps are available for those assigned to unfamiliar territory. A large master map is located in the office.

The minister then thanks the chairperson, core group and entire committee, calling for applause. An opportunity is given for questions. The meeting is dismissed with prayer before 2:00 p.m.

The minister and chairperson need to recognize that this period with the visitors is one of the most significant happenings in the life of the church. The most active lay people are present. Here is a great potential force brought together to challenge fellow members. Challengers also need to be challenged. Spiritual motivation is extremely important. Actually, the budget is met by what happens in this particular gathering! What these key people do with their pledges determines the financial success or failure of the canvass. Through training, they become the heart of the church's

43

stewardship and mission. This meeting can change the life of a congregation and move it forward significantly on every front. Inspired visitors express their commitment in what they say on Visitation Sunday and by what they do on Loyalty Sunday.

As indicated elsewhere, callers' homes are not visited. The material they are taking to others has already been mailed to them. Some churches ask the callers to make a pledge before going out on assignment. The method has merit. They invite others to do what they have already done. On the other hand, the corporate experience of everyone pledging on Loyalty Sunday has great meaning. Variations may be adapted yearly until a church finds its own style.

While the training period is in progress, core committee members are completing final details. Last minute alterations are inevitable. Many worshipers, following the morning service, will indicate they have had a change of plans and will not be home. Their call card needs to be removed, name deleted from the half-sheet and packet set aside for mailing. Quiet preparations continue during the presentation. When assignments are called for, everything is ready and current.

• 7 •

THE VISITORS REPORT BACK

THE PASTOR and other assigned personnel need to be present from 3:00 p.m. until 8:00 p.m. when the callers report back. This is an important part of the canvass. The pulse of the congregation has been fingered. The health of the whole church is reflected in these reports. What is the congregation thinking and feeling? What are their attitudes? What are they saying and what do they want heard? What happens on Loyalty Sunday is the objective response of many individuals. The reporting process is the subjective response of many people.

Returning visitors bring their call lists, packets not delivered and 3 x 5 cards with comments. A simple routine is followed. The debriefer asks for the number listed on the half-sheet and then produces a duplicate from the numbered pile at hand. He or she goes over the calls with the visitor writing opposite each name: "completed," "will call back tomorrow," or "mail." The debriefer destroys the visitor's half-sheet and keeps a duplicate, just marked, in a separate pile. These provide a double check for the office when mailing undelivered packets on Tuesday.

45

After this procedure the caller discusses 3 x 5 card notations. Each person brings useful information: illnesses, problems, requests for material, constructive criticisms, etc. There are also responses to savor when members indicate satisfaction and pleasure with program, worship and mission. All cards need to be carefully evaluated for appropriate action. The visitors are eager to discuss their calls. They have entered into the spirit of the program and see it as a total experience, not just a request for pledges. Perceptive callers detect other areas of stewardship possibilities: musical abilities, teaching interests and readiness to be involved in various programs. Often they stimulate affirmative responses and want to discuss what they have done. Others indicate a personal commitment to follow up on a delinquent family or aid in a particular situation.

These callers are enthusiastic about what they have accomplished or plan to do. Many talk about their own fulfillment through this kind of enterprise. It becomes a tremendous experience for callers and those visited. The whole church is in conversation in one day and the results are truly amazing.

Later in the evening a tired but thoughtful pastor reflects on everything that has happened. He or she gives thanks for dedicated lay people who have put their faith in action and witnessed in the name of Christ. They have been extensions of their pastor—listening—sharing—reaching out—encouraging—comforting—and informing. Their valuable insights will now strengthen a renewed and improved ministry which manifests itself to the entire church family. "Blest be the tie that binds our hearts in Christian love. . . ."

Two or three days after Visitation Sunday send a letter of appreciation to all workers.

Dear Friend:

Please accept my sincere thanks for a splendid church-wide visitation on November 1. You put your stewardship in action for your church. This has been a meaningful experience for all of us.

The results of the visitation have been outstanding. Members have expressed a genuine appreciation and enthusiasm for the calls you made. We are following up on every card where you indicated, for one reason or another, a contact should be made.

I am sure you all sense anew what is happening in the life of our congregation. Please know that you have had a significant part in this forward thrust. May the fine experience of Sunday characterize our churchmanship throughout the year. John Jones, our canvass chairman, joins me in expressing gratitude for your excellent work.

Faithfully yours,

William R. Smith
Minister

P.S. I trust we'll have 100 percent attendance on Loyalty Sunday, November 8, by those who took part in the visitation.

On the Wednesday following Visitation Sunday, packets are mailed to those not home. A secretary opens the sealed packet containing church budget, inspirational brochure and personal pledge card. A new packet is addressed. The material is placed in a letter (see below), inserted in the new packet, sealed and mailed. One of two things happens with every packet: it is either delivered in person or returned to the church for mailing. Every packet must be accounted for since it contains privileged information (typed pledge card). Accuracy in handling is absolutely essential to keep faith with the people.

Dear Friends in First Church:

In preparation for Loyalty Sunday, November 8, enthusiastic visitors called on all members to talk about the budget and program for the coming year. The caller was unable to see you last Sunday so the message could not be given personally. Please accept this letter, however, as a personal call from one of your fellow members.

Our program continues to move forward on every front in a dynamic way. In order to become what we were intended to be and do what we must do, we shall need the continued financial support of every member for 19__.

Enclosed is material which will interest you. Please read it thoroughly. Review your giving to the church honestly and sincerely. Note that the budget has been increased by $____ for 19__. Hopefully every member will show enlarged concern through increased giving.

Your pledge card is also enclosed. Consider prayerfully what you can do for God's work in the coming year and *present your pledge at the Loyalty Worship Service next Sunday, November 8*. If you are unable to attend please mail your pledge card at once.

The work we are able to do next year depends on your proportionate response. Let's make Loyalty Sunday a day of Dedicated Partnership,

The Visitors Report Back

with every member present and every member pledging. November 8 is the day!

Sincerely yours,

John R. Jones, Chairman
Every-Member-Visitation

• 8 •

LOYALTY SUNDAY

LOYALTY SUNDAY is observed the second week in November. Through the years this has become a fixed and important date in the life of the congregation.

Worship for the day needs careful planning and preparation. It is an exciting and inspiring celebration as well as a meaningful and motivating experience. Attendance will be substantially larger than usual. Alter the service allowing for extra music and a special pledging ceremony. Change the bulletin stock and ink color. Devote a generous portion of the bulletin to stewardship. Emphasize the significance of pledging. Mention the successful Visitation Sunday and thank members for their cooperation. All choirs should be used on Loyalty Sunday. Many parents will be present to hear their children sing. Massed choirs also give visibility to something the people support through their giving. Many voices add to the celebration. Select anthems carefully. Sing about the church and its world mission. Use banners. Have a procession. Preach about the spiritual and theological implications of stewardship. Hold before the congregation their responsibility for continued personal growth through giving.

After the sermon say something about "Worship Through Pledging." The offering has previously been received, put in the office, and plates returned to the ushers. At offertory time the minister announces that only the regular tithes and gifts of the people are being received. It is requested that pledges be held for dedication following the sermon. When the sermon is finished the pastor says with confidence and enthusiasm (list in bulletin as Worship Through Pledging):

1. Loyalty Sunday is our opportunity to worship through pledging.
2. What First Church does in 19_, in this community, in the United States and its possessions, and throughout the world, depends on what our congregation does today.
3. All members and friends of First Church have received copies of the proposed budget for 19_, through which the tremendous task and challenge has been presented.
4. Pledge cards and pencils are in the pew racks for those who may have misplaced theirs.
5. Friends of First Church may also make a pledge for 19_ and participate in the on-going program and work of this congregation.
6. Before performing the act of loyalty, let us read together the Prayer of Consecration in your bulletin. (The following prayer, printed in the bulletin, is read in unison.)

O God, our gracious and generous Father, we gratefully acknowledge your ownership and recognize our stewardship. All we have is a trust from you. We thank you that through Christ's love, we have learned the relationship between

51

giving and living. Teach us to give as loyal part-
ners with him. We would pledge to you, an
honorable share of our income. May our pledges
express our genuine love, sincere faith, and true
loyalty. Use us and our offerings to extend the
world-wide kingdom of him who loved us and
gave himself for us. In his name we pray and
pledge. Amen.

7. At this time I shall ask the ushers to come forward and wait on you, as you give your pledge
to your church, and with it yourself, your soul
and body, in renewed consecration to Christ's
cause.

While the choir sings an anthem, the ushers
collect the pledges. The congregation rises for
the Doxology when ushers come forward. A
Prayer of Dedication is read in unison (also
printed in the bulletin).

Heavenly Father, giver of all good things, who
has shown us that it is more blessed to give than
to receive, we dedicate these pledges to the
service of your church, humbly praying that all
our gifts and energies may be dedicated to the
extension of your kingdom on earth. May what
we now cast upon the waters, return to you, for
the strengthening of our congregation, the
nurture of fellowmen, and to the everlasting
glory of your name—for the sake of Jesus Christ.
Amen.

Immediately following the prayer, the organ
begins the closing hymn: "All Hail the Power of
Jesus' Name." In triumphant song this meaningful service is brought to a stirring climax. Planning, prayer, hard work and thoughtful
preparation all culminate in a moving spiritual
experience.

Loyalty Sunday

As mentioned earlier, a substantial part of the bulletin is devoted to the stewardship message. The basic material shown below speaks to the entire congregation.

LOYALTY SUNDAY TODAY
EVERY-MEMBER-PLEDGING FOR 19_

invest In HOPE,   **STEP**
By
step

What the members of the church do today will test their love of God, loyalty to Christ, and sincerity toward the church. It will determine whether we can carry the great responsibilities that go with the increasing mission of First Church. It will be indicative of the effectiveness of First Church's service. It will prove our awareness of the need of the nation and the world for what Christians have to offer. The official boards propose a minimum budget of $_____. There is no limit to what our church can do. What we will let our church do in 19_ is answered in our pledges and by our continuing loyalty.

MY PLEDGE

MY pledge is an expression of my loyalty to my church.

MY pledge is an open confession that I believe in orderly methods of sharing in my church obligation and do so with integrity.

MY pledge is a revelation of my faith in the Gospel of Christ in bringing the Kingdom of God on earth.

MY pledge is my response to the call in the world around me for love and light and peace.

MY pledge, together with those of my fellow members, reveals the moral strength and spiritual awareness of my church.

MY pledge represents the value and worth which I attach to my religion.

AN EXCITING DAY—Last Sunday. That was the report brought back by lay people of the church who called in the homes of the congregation. These loyal and enthusiastic people freely gave their time to tell the story of the forward movement of the church. Members of the congregation received them with graciousness and courtesy. Truly it was a thrilling day in the life of our corporate family. An expression of thanks is extended to the visitors for their time, the congregation for their cooperation and Mr. John Jones and the Every-Member-Visitation Committee for their planning.

Following the Loyalty Sunday service, at a mutually convenient time, the core committee meets to alphabetize pledge cards, convert weekly figures into a yearly amount and to total. Use two adding machines. One person takes half of the cards. A second person takes the other half. Alternate the process. Both sets of figures should match for both sets of cards. If not, carefully double check. An accurate total is imperative at the beginning. Subsequent amounts are built on the initial base.

Up to 80 percent of the pledges arrive by Loyalty Sunday. Some have already come by mail. Place cards in the following categories: Adult Members, Non-members, Youth Budget, College and No Pledge. There are people who will not sign a pledge but indicate they will contribute regularly by using envelopes. This is a form of pledge. These people are not included in follow-up mail or calls. Begin a cumulative record for yearly comparison. A sample format follows.

Loyalty Sunday, November 8, 19__
___ Member pledges ....$____
___ Non-member pledges ... ____
___ Youth pledges .... ____
___ College pledges .... ____
___ No pledge .... ____

TOTAL $____

Continue the process each week until all the cards are in. Show totals regularly in the bulletin. This indicates progress and serves as a reminder to those who have not pledged. A weekly paragraph in the bulletin might read:

PROGRESS REPORT ON LOYALTY SUN-DAY. ___ pledges have been received with a total pledged for 19__ of $_____ toward the goal of $_____. Children and youth have pledged $_____ to the Youth Budget which is included in the total listed above. A number of pledges are still to be returned. It is urgent that every pledge be in promptly. Let us have every member pledging for 19__. Non-members are also invited to share in our goals for the coming year. Make your pledge today if you have not already done so and place on the offering plate. Pledge cards are available in the pew racks.

It has been noted elsewhere that two sets of 3 x 5 cards must be prepared for every family unit in the congregation. One set is used by callers for recording their visits. The other set (colored) identifies those who have not pledged. A secretary removes the corresponding card for each pledge received. Those left indicate the names of members who have made no response. As pledge cards are received by mail, brought to the office, or returned the following Sunday(s), the colored card is removed from the file. The remaining colored cards show the amount of follow-up that needs to be done.

· 9 ·

FOLLOW-UP

FOLLOW-UP is essential in every canvass. No matter how well the target date (Loyalty Sunday) has been publicized, there are always those who have trouble meeting deadlines. Some may have reservations and need further encouragement. Others are careless about obligations, poorly organized, or indifferent. There are many degrees of priority in every congregation. Follow-up is necessary for maximum participation and response.

Follow-up style can change from year to year. Unquestionably, the most effective method is personal visitation. With the type of canvass program we have outlined, a core group of experienced visitors has already been established as the follow-up committee. They are the recruiters who secure the callers, serve as substitutes on Visitation Sunday and have already accepted responsibility for follow-up. This group can be supplemented with church officers and volunteers who signed up on Visitation Sunday. The follow-up should take place one or two weeks after Loyalty Sunday. A letter is sent to

the recruiters and other volunteers, the Tuesday
after Loyalty Sunday, asking them to be present
on the day selected:

> Dear Friend:
> We are grateful for your willingness to
> participate in the Every-Member-Visitation
> Follow-Up. It is important that we contact those
> members who have not pledged.
>
> Please come to the church on Sunday, Novem-
> ber —, at 3:30 p.m. for a short meeting in the
> Parlor. At that time calls will be assigned and
> there will be a helpful briefing.
>
> You will have one week in which to complete
> your calls. Our meeting should be completed by
> 4:15 p.m. You may choose to begin your work
> immediately.
>
> Sincerely,
>
> John R. Jones, Chairman
> Every-Member-Visitation

Following the service on the third or fourth
Sunday, the financial secretary immediately
removes from the file the colored 3 x 5 card for
each pledge received that morning. The remaining cards indicate the number and names of
non-pledgers. A duplicate card is made for use
by follow-up visitors. The minister and canvass
chairperson review those to be visited. Some
may be removed for particular reasons: extended
vacation, hospitalization, other problems.
Although the process is systematic there also
needs to be sensitivity and selectivity. Place
cards on tables so that follow-up people may
select the calls they choose to make. If some
desire to visit people they know, this should be

an option. Many have no preference and wish to be assigned.

When the callers are assembled, the minister talks with them about the nature and type of contact to be made. They are reminded that those to be visited have had full information about the importance of commitment. Encouragement is given to approach the task with Christian grace and understanding. Extra pledge cards are provided along with a small envelope (3½ x 6) imprinted with: "My Pledge to My Church." People can make an immediate pledge and place it in the sealed envelope, which is returned by the caller. Visitors are given one week to complete their task. Before they leave, ask them to list the names they have selected or been assigned. This record is kept at the church. If a pledge comes to the office by mail during the week, the visitor is notified and no follow-up is necessary.

On the Wednesday following Loyalty Sunday, a letter is sent to those members who have not returned their pledges. It is a gracious communication suggesting another target date. Notification is also given that officers and visitors will call on those who have not responded by the third Sunday of November.

> Dear Fellow Member:
> This letter comes as reminder that your pledge for the year 19_ has not been received. In case you have misplaced yours, we are taking the liberty of enclosing another.
> Loyalty Sunday was a thrilling experience. There is a spirit of enthusiasm sweeping through our church which is most significant.

We trust that you sense the unusual progress that has been made and the potential for growth and expansion.

That is why we need the loyalty and support of every member. The vows of church membership express the affirmation of personal sharing on a regular basis.

Please return your pledge by Sunday, November 15. Either mail it before that date or bring it with you to the worship service. *Officers and visitors from the church will call on all members who have not turned in pledge cards, on the afternoon of November 15.*

Your church is, and can become, only what you want it to be through your interest, support, and loyalty. A great year lies ahead as we work together in serving our Lord.

Sincerely,

John R. Jones, Chairman
Every-Member-Visitation

· 10 ·

MAIL FOLLOW-UP

SOME churches may prefer to follow up by using a series of letters. Others may choose personal calling one year and mail the next. Promptness of response varies from congregation to congregation. Also, each church or community has a distinctive personality. Some areas may have competing pressures (such as United Fund) during the canvass period. These factors need to be recognized by the canvass committee because they can affect personal attitudes. People resist too much pressure in too short a period. Increasingly, individuals are reacting to the many causes urging voluntary contributions. They may want to have a part in all of them, but need time to decide. Others simply procrastinate. Weigh and consider the various components. A spaced, mail follow-up may be a firm but less pressured approach.

Following the third Sunday in November, use the letter that appears at the end of the previous chapter. Change the fourth paragraph to read:

> Please return your pledge by Sunday, November 29, and let it be an expression of your thanksgiving to God for all his blessings. We

need your assistance now in order to make plans
for the coming year.

If there is no response another letter is mailed
early in December. (A sample follows.) Note the
third paragraph. Before such a statement can be
made, the "carry-over concept" has to be
thoroughly considered by the official board(s) of
the church. The matter should be covered early
in September, when the boards discuss the projected budget and approve the dates and type of
canvass.

Although this is a valid assumption, there are
some dangers. Many people consistently over-
pledge, under-achieve, or neglect to honor their
pledge. Therefore, the financial secretary needs
to review carefully the names of those receiving
the carry-over letter. The secretary learns to
know the habits and patterns of all donors. Experience may dictate that certain persons should
not be committed to carry-over. An unreliable
budget projection could result, with serious
ramifications later in the year. Send them the
same letter shown below, with the third paragraph deleted. If they make a pledge response, it
is safe to assume they will do better, though still
inconsistent, than if carried-over.

Dear Fellow Member:
We need your help! It has been nearly two
months since Loyalty Sunday and we have not
heard from you regarding your pledge to First
Church. Since it is necessary to make our
budget preparations for 19_, we need a response
from every member.
It would be greatly appreciated if you would
return your pledge by December 12. Either mail

it before that date or bring it with you to the worship service. In case you have misplaced yours, we are taking the liberty of sending another.

IF YOUR PLEDGE CARD IS NOT RE-CEIVED IN THE OFFICE BY DECEMBER 12, IT WILL BE ASSUMED THAT YOU DESIRE YOUR 19_ PLEDGE TO CONTINUE FOR 19_. THEREFORE, THE OFFICERS OF THE CHURCH HAVE INSTRUCTED THE FINANCIAL SECRETARY TO CARRY FOR-WARD 19_ PLEDGES INTO 19_, WHER-EVER A NEW PLEDGE HAS NOT BEEN MADE.

19_ promises to be a challenging and fruitful year. We are grateful for your support in the past. Let us look forward to the future of our church with enthusiasm and continue to strengthen it with our love and loyalty.

Sincerely yours,

John R. Jones, Chairman
Every-Member-Visitation

Signed pledges may still result from the carry-over letter. Some may be the same as the previous year or even lower. However, a new pledge has been made. This is a more reliable indication of intent. Others may increase their pledge, having planned it that way, but simply being slow to respond. If within ten days there are no telephone calls or notes reacting to the carry-over letter, it is safe to assume that silence is acceptance. Therefore, the financial secretary removes the colored card from the follow-up file and makes out a regular pledge card for the current amount. The colored card, with a notation that the carry-over letter was sent, is stapled to the back of the pledge card. Later, if someone calls to question the matter, the colored card is an indication that they received a carry-over letter.

Near the end of the year it will be noted that some colored cards still remain in the uncompleted file. Previous mailings and dates are recorded on all cards. Often these are individuals who are drifting toward the periphery of commitment and responsibility. Nevertheless, they are still members of the church. They need to be reminded of their obligation to keep faith with fellow members who consistently support the church. Make no apology for being persistent. This is the third communication since Loyalty Sunday. Offering envelopes have already been mailed.

Dear Fellow Member:

By now you have already received your church offering envelopes for the year 19_. Although you have not made a specific pledge for the new year, the envelopes are for your use in making recordable contributions to your church.

As was indicated when you voluntarily joined this congregation, and through subsequent information, one of the obligations of church membership is financial support. This is established by the Constitution of our denomination (or church bylaws) as a personal requirement for each individual.

Many times members are unaware of the fact that there is a cost to the church for every person listed on the rolls. This amounts to approximately $15.00 per year, per person. It includes mailed materials, postage, handling, oversight of church rolls and per capita apportionment. The per capita apportionment (tax) is levied for every member by Presbytery, Synod, and General Assembly (conference, district, etc.) and in 19_ amounts to $_ per member. All quotas and goals for mission giving and emergency appeals are based on membership count.

As long as you continue to be a member of First Church, we would lovingly remind you of your minimum fair part in fulfilling the obligations to which the church is committed on your behalf. When not fulfilled, it means that someone else in the congregation, along with their own fair share, is helping to carry the fair share of others.

This letter comes as information regarding the budget which is related to the number of members on the record. The officers of First Church have asked that this communication be sent as an indication of their care and concern.

Sincerely yours,

William K. Franklin
Treasurer

A second contact is also necessary for out-of-town members. They received an initial letter well in advance of Loyalty Sunday reminding them of their "active" relationship to the home church, even though they now live in another community. Included was a pledge card, copy of the budget, inspirational material and a request to return the pledge before November 8. A final paragraph encouraged transfer if they had found a new church home. Within two weeks of Loyalty Sunday, if they have not pledged, another contact should be made encouraging specific action: support or transfer.

Dear Friend:

This letter comes as a reminder that your pledge for 19_ has not been received by the church. In case you have misplaced yours, we are taking the liberty of sending another.

THE ART OF CHURCH CANVASS

Loyalty Sunday on November 8 was a thrilling day! There is a genuine spirit of enthusiasm sweeping through our church. We wish you might be closer to us, in terms of miles, so that you could share in a personal way this wonderful vitality.

However, you can have a real part in what your church is doing through your financial support. We need the concern and loyalty of every member. The vows of church membership express the affirmation that each person will contribute to the church on a regular basis.

Whether a resident or non-resident member, the responsibility remains the same. Until such time as you find a church home in your locality, we know that as a conscientious Christian you will want to fulfill your vows by supporting your home church.

May we hear from you in the very near future about your pledge? If, in the meantime, you have decided on a new church home, please advise us and we will transfer your membership.

Sincerely yours,

John R. Jones, Chairman
Every-Member-Visitation

· 11 ·

OTHER LETTERS

LETTERS have a vital role in the successful canvass. They condition, inform, publicize and stimulate. Wording is very important. Timing is also essential in setting the pace. Certain key concepts such as loyalty, commitment, obligation, responsibility and involvement need to be emphasized and repeated.

One of the initial communications is directed to out-of-town members. They are not included in the 3 x 5 cards because personal calling is not involved. Make a special list of all those living out of canvass range. The epistle shown below is gracious and friendly, telling about visitation and Loyalty Sunday. It purposely assumes continued commitment.

Dear Fellow Member:

Your church continues to throb with vitality! I say "your church," for although you live in another community, you have chosen to keep your relationship here. As long as you remain a member, you are still a definite part of this church and its program. We have appreciated your commitment in the past. We know that you will want to support your church, in a realistic way, during the coming year.

If you were still living in _____, you would be regular in your attendance at worship. On Sunday afternoon, November 1, a visitor would call on you to talk about Christian stewardship. This letter comes in place of a call.

Enclosed please find material telling of the growing program at First Church. Please read it thoughtfully. Note the proposed budget and our concern for mission. You can share in our task and responsibility even though the miles may separate us.

Please think and pray about your stewardship. Then mail your pledge card as soon as possible. Sunday, November 8, is Loyalty Sunday when all pledges will be dedicated during morning worship. Join us in spirit on that special day.

If you have found a church home in your new locality please let us know and we shall transfer your membership. Until such time, we shall count on your loyalty to First Church.

Sincerely yours,

John R. Jones, Chairman
Every-Member-Visitation

Perhaps the single most important letter of the whole canvass is the one mailed to the entire congregation (except college students and out-of-town members). This communication sets the stewardship scene, informs members about visitation, and points up the meaning of Loyalty Sunday. The sample below contains the basic elements. The last four paragraphs can stay essentially the same from year to year. Annual emphasis should be reflected in the first two or three paragraphs.

STEP
share Your LOVE,   By
step

68

Other Letters

YOU ARE PART OF THE WHOLE MISSION
OF CHRIST AND HIS CHURCH

Dear Fellow Member:

We are called upon to give as God has given to us. This is the standard of giving the Bible teaches . . . planned, purposeful, and proportionate giving. For faithful Christians there can be no other way. Giving isn't a matter of occasional impulse. It's a measure of our faithfulness and of our obedience to Christ.

We are grateful for the growing number of First Church members who think in terms of percentages and are continuing to raise their giving to a minimum of 5 percent of family income. At the same time we are grateful for the substantial number of fellow members, thinking percentages, who are concentrating on the tithe (10 percent of income) or beyond, as an expression of personal faith.

Such commitment has affected the life of this congregation significantly. The mark of a living church is the size of its benevolent heart. Christian nurture is taking place. God is blessing us to become a blessing, beginning here in _____, and extending through the whole world.

In Christian optimism, the officers of First Church are proposing a carefully studied, thoroughly documented and realistically possible budget for 19__, in the amount of $____. This is an increase of $____ over 19__ (__ percent). Let us join together as a congregation and share our love in ministry and mission.

VISITATION DAY IS SUNDAY, NOVEMBER 1. On that day all homes will be visited by church callers. They will talk with you about your church and its program, leaving illustrative literature and your pledge card. We know you will greet your fellow members with Christian courtesy. Please plan to be home between 2:00 p.m. and 5:00 p.m. to receive the caller.

LOYALTY SUNDAY IS NOVEMBER 8. LET

69

EVERY MEMBER BE PRESENT ON THIS MEANINGFUL DAY! Pledge cards will be presented and dedicated at the worship service. No member will want to miss this hour when we indicate our involvement in the whole mission of the church at home and abroad. If it is absolutely impossible for you to be present on November 8, please mail your pledge card before that date for the Service of Dedication. CONSIDER YOUR STEWARDSHIP CAREFULLY AND PRAYERFULLY! Renewal through stewardship comes as we find the joy of giving and partnership through sharing. Loyalty Sunday is the day when we say by what we do: "Let the church take a giant STEP FORWARD . . . and count on me!"

Your in His Service

Mary L. Smith, Chairperson
Interpretation and Stewardship

College students living at home or away at school receive a conversational communication offering some options. Young people who have been part of the church's youth budget training program should have the opportunity to continue their financial relationship, even though on a limited basis. The church that does not challenge its students to a stewardship discipline withholds part of its continuing nurture. Many students write warm personal letters expressing gratitude for their church relationship. Collegiate giving can be surprisingly substantial, particularly if there is a community college in the area or a city university. This means that many college people are living at home and have fairly good jobs while attending school full or part time. No follow-up letter is sent, since these people are more sensitive to pressure and are still undecided as to eventual location.

Dear Student:

Please accept this letter as a personal visit. By reading the enclosed material you can sense the continued growth taking place in First Church.

We know that as a member you will want to have a share in its forward thrust. All young people attending school are being invited to make a student pledge. This may be only a token amount, but it still represents your interest in the church and concern for its program.

Those of you away at school may want to give your gift all at once. You can also place your offering in an envelope marked with your name, during those times you worship when at home. Those of you living in the community and worshiping regularly may desire regular offering envelopes.

Every student is faced with the costliness of an education. Each cent counts, as the church well knows. Money priorities are seen in the perspective of needs and goals. At the same time, any gift has significant meaning. Sharing with your church is showing love and concern for the value of the church in our society.

We wish you every choice blessing during the academic year. Your church stands ready to serve you in any way possible. Pray for us, even as we pray for you.

Sincerely yours,

Mary L. Smith, Chairperson
Interpretation and Stewardship

P. S. Loyalty Sunday is November 8. If you wish to make a Student Pledge, it should be in by that time for the Service of Dedication.

The young adult missive is an optional form designed for unmarried high school or college graduates. In some situations where a twenty-year-old person lives at home and works, the canvasser will contact that person along with his or her parents on Visitation Sunday. However, there are other situations in which a personal visit on Sunday afternoon may be rather difficult. This would be true where working girls live in a women's apartment complex or where several young men may rent or own a house together. Some circumstances in the present social scene would prevent a constructive and comfortable visit on the part of the caller. The young adult letter can be used in place of a call. This does get the packet and pledge card to the individual. And it eliminates some difficult calling situations.

> Dear Young Adult:
>
> Please accept this letter as a personal visit. Enclosed you will find material telling of the growth, progress, and needs of First Church. As a member of the congregation, we ask your continued loyalty and support in the tremendous program for which we have responsibility in the community, nation and world.
>
> We would urge you to take your part in the life of our church along with many children, youth and adults who are making possible these significant developments. The church needs your enthusiasm, commitment, talent and financial support.
>
> We invite you to share in the present and for the future through your giving to First Church. Enclosed is your pledge card. When signed, it is your expression of love, gratitude and concern. Pause prayerfully and sign thoughtfully.

72

No one will call on you November 1, but we urge you to be in church on Sunday, November 8, which is Loyalty Sunday. At that time we will dedicate our pledges to the Glory of God. If you cannot be present please mail your pledge before that date. United in common cause for a common Lord, let us help our particular church minister more effectively by the tangible expression of our inner convictions.

Sincerely yours,

Mary L. Smith, Chairperson
Interpretation and Stewardship

Many people are related to the local church in various ways, but have never formally become members. Some are regular in attendance and support, but keep their membership in a church back home where they might eventually retire. Others send their children to church school and occasionally worship. Some have their children enrolled in the choir program. Many are future prospects. There are also those who form comfortable relationships with certain areas of congregational life but do not want to commit themselves to formal membership. They may have an associate involvement with a woman's circle, retired people's group, etc. These individuals are part of the larger family of the particular parish. They should have the opportunity of taking part in the whole mission of the church. Many support quite generously by making a pledge and/or using offering envelopes. Each year an invitation should be extended. This is an area for cultivation that must not be overlooked.

THE ART OF CHURCH CANVASS

Dear Friend of First Church:

We know that you are interested in our church and its program because you are associated with it directly or indirectly. We covet this interest and pray that the church may be a blessing to you. We seek to serve you in any way possible.

Pledges are now being gathered for the financial support of our work in 19__. Included with this letter is material telling of our significant Christian program. We urge you to read it. You will also find a proposed minimum budget and we would like to invite you to share in it, if you so desire.

We have included a pledge card. Through a pledge to First Church you can join us in promoting the work of Christ's kingdom at home and abroad. Loyalty Sunday, November 8, is the time we are bringing our pledge cards to the worship service for dedication. We extend an invitation to join in this experience with us. Or, if you wish, you may mail your pledge to the church office.

The program here is making a great impact on the community. In order to expand and increase its outreach and growth, we are looking to all who are touched by this church in any way, to aid its effectiveness. We are grateful for every expression of support.

Cordially yours,

Mary L. Smith, Chairperson
Interpretation and Stewardship

P. S. If you would prefer offering envelopes without making a pledge, please indicate and we shall be happy to supply you with a set. Envelopes are automatically sent to all who make pledges.

• 12 •

COMMUNICATIONS ABOUT
THE CANVASS

COMMUNICATION keeps the canvass operating smoothly. When the recruiters call back to the church office, a "yes" or "no" is placed opposite each name on their assignment. This of course indicates whether or not a person plans to visit on November 1. A letter from the church must be sent confirming the verbal agreement. It contains an expression of thanks for willingness to service, information about the meal and training on that particular Sunday, and notification that homes of callers will not be visited. With this communication the callers receive a packet containing material they will deliver, as well as their personal pledge card. Each caller now has a pledge card. This is the first phase of local distribution.

> Dear Friend:
>
> Thank you for responding to the call to serve in our every-home-visitation on Sunday, November 1. This will be a rich and rewarding experience. It offers a great opportunity to demonstrate our enthusiasm for the work of Christ's church.
>
> On Sunday, November 1, at 12:30 p.m. we shall meet in Fellowship Hall for a complimentary dinner. Please pick up your prepared name tag

at the north entrance. Your tag will also indicate table seating.

Instructions and material will be given at dinner. Following that, we make our visits to the homes of members. You will need your own transportation. Each person will go singly unless otherwise indicated. There will be four to six calls.

All church members have been asked to remain at home on Sunday afternoon, November 1, until you have called. Our members will be glad to see you. Expect a cordial response. Naturally, since you are a caller, it is understood that your home will not be visited.

Looking forward to seeing you at dinner, I am

Sincerely yours,

John R. Jones, Chairman
Every-Member-Visitation

P.S. INCLUDED WITH THIS LETTER IS YOUR PACKET, WHICH IS THE SAME AS THE ONE YOU WILL DELIVER TO HOMES OF THE CONGREGATION. READ THE MATERIAL CAREFULLY. YOUR OWN PLEDGE CARD IS ALSO ENCLOSED, TO BE RETURNED ON LOYALTY SUNDAY, NOVEMBER 8.

P.P.S. IF YOU CANNOT VISIT ON THE FIRST, DUE TO THE UNEXPECTED, CALL THE OFFICE IMMEDIATELY! WE ARE DEPENDING ON EACH PERSON, AND CALLS ARE ASSIGNED ON THAT BASIS.

Some individuals have to say "no" to the recruiter who invites them to participate. They may have previous commitments, out-of-town involvements or personal complications. Since these are usually active individuals, it is appropriate to send them a word of understanding along

with their packet. Now, the second step in local
distribution is completed.

Dear Fellow Member:

We are sorry that you will not be able to assist
with the Every-Member-Visitation this year.
However, we certainly understand that there are
circumstances and commitments which make it
impossible for you to be with us.

Therefore, we are sending you the information
packet by mail and *no call will be made at your
home.* Every member of the church is receiving
this same material giving insights into the
progress of First Church and the need to increase our stewardship for 19__.

Please read the material carefully. I'm sure that
you continue to sense the spiritual vitality that is
everywhere evident in the life of our congregation. I am certain, too, that you realize the importance of making the work of our church
increasingly effective here at home and abroad.

Make every effort to be in church on *Loyalty
Sunday, November 8.* Pledge cards (you will
find yours in the packet) will be returned at that
time for a special Service of Dedication. If you
are unable to be present, please mail your
pledge to the office. Thank you for your continued interest in and support of the work of
your church.

Sincerely yours,

John R. Jones, Chairman
Every-Member-Visitation

The next communication has many uses and
was devised to cover various special circumstances. In every congregation there are loyal
members who are uncomfortable with the canvass. Some have been nurtured on sacrificial
stewardship and feel a canvass is unnecessary.
They have their point, as well as their strong

THE ART OF CHURCH CANVASS

feelings. To spare an embarrassing situation with a caller and to respect their point of view, the letter shown below can be comfortably used. It also gets the pledge card delivered.

Some may live at locations too difficult to find conveniently. People may go into the hospital just before Visitation Sunday. Others may be in rest homes, where it is psychologically difficult to make a call. Yet, they want to be included in the whole life of the church and would be upset if they did not receive a pledge card. There are varying circumstances too numerous to mention. This letter covers a multitude of unusual situations. It should be sent a day or two after the all-church communication, mentioned in the previous chapter. Their 3 x 5 card has been removed in anticipation of sending mail. The minister or canvass chairperson decides on the recipients.

Dear Fellow Member:

We are grateful for your continued loyalty to the work and program of First Church. In order to simplify the vast work of the Visitation Committee, we are taking the liberty of sending you the information packet by mail. *No call will be made at your home on Visitation Sunday, November 1.*

Every member of the church is receiving this same material giving insights into the progress of First Church and the increased needs of 19__.

I'm sure that you continue to sense the spiritual vitality that is everywhere evident in the life of our congregation. I am certain, too, that you realize the importance of making the work of our church increasingly effective here at home and abroad.

Communications About the Canvass

Make every effort to be in church on *Loyalty Sunday, November 8.* Pledge cards (you will find yours in the packet) will be returned at that time for a special Service of Dedication. If you are unable to be present, please mail your pledge to the office. Thank you for your continued interest in and support of the work of your church.

Sincerely yours,

John R. Jones, Chairman
Every-Member-Visitation

Upon receipt of the all-congregation notification about Visitation Sunday, many conscientious members call the office indicating they will not be at home. The packet and pledge card still need to reach them. The letter below adds a personal touch.

Dear Fellow Member:

Thank you for the courtesy of letting us know that you do not plan to be home on Visitation Sunday, November 1.

This is the material the caller would have delivered. Please read it carefully. I'm sure that you continue to sense the spiritual vitality present in our congregational life. I am certain, too, that you realize the importance of making the work of our church increasingly effective at home and abroad.

Please make every effort to be in church on *Loyalty Sunday, November 8.* Pledge cards will be returned at that time for a special Service of Dedication. If you are unable to be present, please mail your pledge in advance of that date. Thank you for your continued interest in the work of First Church.

Sincerely yours,

John R. Jones, Chairman
Every-Member-Visitation

79

• 13 •

A CONTINUING CANVASS

THE Every-Member-Canvass is a major event in any congregation. We have been talking about those factors involved in a particular undertaking. Actually, the canvass continues to operate in different ways throughout the year. This is especially true in regard to new members.

One of the questions asked of those who join the church is: "Will you support the church to the best of your ability?" Therefore, Christian stewardship must be included in new member training. In teaching the class, the pastor needs to discuss the theological implications of time, talents and money. Those present can be confronted with the claims of spiritual sharing in a way that is not always possible from the pulpit or by letter. In this setting people ought to be challenged to grow from childhood concepts to mature commitment. Various items of literature can be made available stressing dimensions of local congregation outreach as well as denominational mission. Along with that material, a statement about responsible support should be given to each person joining the church:

A Continuing Canvass

FIRST CHURCH OF _____

Our Philosophy of Financial Support

When you promise financial support to First Church

1. You are fulfilling a part of your membership vows: "Do you promise to give of your substance as the Lord may prosper you?"
2. The pledge card you will receive after you join the church is a record of your intended investment. It is a voluntary statement of your commitment upon which your church bases its expenditures, makes its plans and carries forward its total program.
3. Your "investment" may be raised or lowered as your financial circumstances change significantly. One needs only to call the financial secretary and adjustments will be made in a courteous and confidential manner.
4. You will be participating in a truly Christian plan of financial giving. This is called proportionate giving. All gifts are given in proportion to one's worldly means: "... in proportion as the Lord may prosper you." Often, as a first-time venture in systematic giving, people begin with 2 percent or 3 percent of income as their proportion. As spiritual concern and maturity develop the percentage can also voluntarily increase to 5 percent and eventually to 10 percent, known as the Tithe.
5. The Church of Jesus Christ is a significant enterprise. What the church does, its members make possible through their prayers, service and tangible support of the program. The vast and far-flung areas of spiritual concern at home and abroad are maintained by the sacrificial sharing of those who are deeply concerned in the Christian sense of the word.
6. You will be given offering envelopes, for they make all gifts equal in the sight of men. All pledges are held in strictest confidence.
7. The church budget is arranged in three categories: Local Mission (for the work of the local

81

church), General Mission (for the work of the church world-wide) and Capital Funds (for the on-going physical improvement of our building). One total pledge is made and the Trustees use all income on a proportionate basis.

8. You are assured of a policy of limited special offerings, which must first be approved by the officers.

9. In considering a total pledge to the church one should keep in mind that children and youth are invited to contribute to the Youth Budget as a method of developing good stewardship habits while in church school. Also, our Association of Church Women does not engage in fund-raising activities such as bazaars, carnivals or bake sales. The Association work is supported by the pledges of members. Therefore, when making a pledge to the church, take into consideration the above factors.

10. You will receive a financial receipt every three months indicating the church's record of your giving. This is not a "bill." Rather, it is an accounting for your own personal files. It indicates the accuracy of church records and perhaps, at times, may be a friendly reminder.

THE CHURCH OF JESUS CHRIST DEPENDS ON DEDICATED, REALISTIC AND LOVING STEWARDSHIP

Two or three days after new members are publicly welcomed at the Sunday service, a letter is sent from the church Treasurer inviting them to make a pledge. Include a copy of the church budget, descriptive literature and a pledge card.

Dear Mr. & Mrs. New Member:

We are happy that you are officially a part of our First Church family and we look forward to your association with us in the great cause of Christ. We trust that you will continue to become in-

A *Continuing Canvass*

creasingly involved in the inspiring fellowship and service of this congregation.

Your church provides an extensive program of worship, education and service to which all faithful members give their liberal and generous support. The Scriptures direct us in matters of giving and indicate that it should be generous, cheerful, systematic and in proportion to income.

You are invited to make a pledge in the form of one amount. The officers then distribute all income through the three areas of the church budget: Local Mission (current expenses), General Mission (benevolences) and Capital Funds (major improvements and mortgage payments). The enclosed budget shows the distribution for the current year.

The church can do only what its members make possible. Every faithful member of First Church makes a worthy weekly pledge. Please fill in the enclosed pledge card and put it on the offering plate next Sunday or return by mail. Your 19_ envelopes are being sent under separate cover.

Our very best wishes to you as you enjoy your membership in First Church. Let us look forward to great things as we share in the on-going program of our church.

Sincerely yours,

Sally R. Smith, Treasurer

Ours is an increasingly transient society. People move more and more frequently. This affects church support. Conscientious individuals often seek out their pastor before a move, asking for guidance on what to do about their pledge. Others are transferred so quickly they have little opportunity to talk about the matter. Some do not even think about it. Nevertheless, the church has a responsibility for informing all communicants

83

regarding membership status when a move takes place. Along with this, some counsel should be given about continuing support.

A personal letter from the pastor can extend a gracious farewell and at the same time remind those who are leaving that they are still members locally until they ask for a transfer. They should be urged to find a new church home and then change their affiliation. Include a paragraph expressing the official position of the denomination or local congregation concerning non-resident members.

The officers should prepare a statement regarding support of the home church by those who move to another community. It can be mimeographed or printed, using the heading: "Pledge Information for Those Who Move." Various options might be suggested. This answers sincere questions and serves as a reminder of financial responsibility. Include the interpretive statement from the official board in the farewell letter.

• 14 •

INSPIRATIONAL AND INTER- PRETIVE MATERIAL

STEWARDSHIP interpretation is not limited to one particular season. It is the continuing task of every church. Aid is provided at the denominational level. Useful materials come at regular intervals highlighting the whole mission of the church. Each week the bulletin can carry lines or paragraphs pointing up items of interest and involvement. If the congregation has actual support of missionaries or a correspondence (Personal Mission Interest) relationship with personnel or projects, these should be listed regularly. Letters from personal mission interests can be posted on bulletin boards or featured in the church newsletter. Many churches include a place during worship for laypeople or pastor to present "A Minute for Mission." This may be varied by the use of cassette tapes with prepared messages. Enhance the church bulletin boards, halls or meeting rooms with inspirational posters. The scope of local, national and world involvement cannot be confined to one particular segment of the ecclesiastical calendar. In many ways, individuals are being conditioned for the canvass throughout the year.

Beginning in late September, complement the regular program of interpretation with additional information. Place inserts in the bulletin each week until canvass. These are obtainable free of charge or at nominal cost from denominational sources. The Louis Neibauer Co. of Ivyland, Pennsylvania prepares some excellent and unusual leaflets for calendar or newsletter enclosure.Professionally designed supplementary stewardship material can greatly enhance the effectiveness of the canvass. Knowing the type of emphasis governs selection and purchase.

Many of the items used will originate locally under the direction of the minister or canvass chairperson. Talent within the congregation can be used for creative writing, design and attractive copy. Careful thought needs to be given to the presentation of the budget itself. Attractive pictures of congregational life give visibility to amounts. Diagrams showing percentage distribution helps in understanding expenditure. Change the format regularly. Use different colored stock and complementary inks, if printed. When mimeographed, include "mime-illustrations" to perk up the presentation.

The Louis Neibauer Co. prepares bulletin stock for stewardship use (8½ x 11) which, when folded, provides three pages for information, plus the pre-designed inspirational front cover. Page two can be used for a message from the pastor or some highly respected member of the congregation. Page three should show the budget. What is said on page two refers to page three, which is visible during the time of reading. A positive statement about commitment should appear on page four. Various types of print can enhance the wording.

Christian Stewardship means taking our religion seriously! What will be your response through the Ministry of Christian Giving?

Here are some principles which will help you reach a decision.

1. A Christian steward prepares personally through WORSHIP and PRAYER.
2. A Christian steward is concerned with translating FAITH into ACTION.
3. A Christian steward REMEMBERS with humility an indebtedness to God.
4. A Christian steward is THOUGHTFUL about the tremendous needs at home and abroad.
5. A Christian steward shows COMPASSION and UNDERSTANDING which are expressed in the QUALITY of giving.
6. A Christian steward makes an HONEST EVALU-ATION of personal income and then makes a REALISTIC PLEDGE.
7. A Christian steward gives SYSTEMATICALLY by pledging a definite amount each week.
8. A Christian steward PLEDGES PROPOR-TIONATELY by setting a PERCENTAGE that expresses partnership.
9. A Christian steward seeks to RAISE the pledge each year in order not to become a STATIC giver.
10. A Christian steward gives GRACIOUSLY, GENEROUSLY AND GRATEFULLY as an expression of thanks to God for His inexpressible gift!

    In order to minister more effectively to the needs of the world and continue an expanding program here at home, First Church members will want to respond to the call to support their

church with INCREASED GIVING AND LOY-
ALTY! We minister in the name of Christ
through our Stewardship
YOUR DECISION ... The proportion You decide
upon is an extension of Your Faith ... The
evidence of Your Involvement ... The Expression of Your Love!
WE GIVE TO GOD *THROUGH* THE BUDGET OF
FIRST CHURCH

The church newsletter is a particularly effective instrument of interpretation for Loyalty Sunday. Depending on when it is published, the
October or November front page features
stewardship.

UPDATING OUR GIVING

The ten-cent cup of coffee has gone the way of
the penny postcard. We cannot mail a postcard
for one cent and we cannot buy a cup of coffee
for a thin dime. We know it. We accept it. We
have adjusted our lives to it. The same with
heating costs, market basket increases and the
price of gasoline. Escalation is the word—rising
from one level to the next.

By the same token, incomes can and do escalate
during the same period in which the penny
postcard escalates from one cent to ten cents.
Some incomes keep pace, some incomes out-
pace escalation, and others may go down, due to
circumstances or fixed pensions. It is interesting,
at this point, to note some figures from the Har-
ris Trust and Savings Bank of Chicago.
"From 1966 to 1976 Median Income is up 100
percent. From 1966 to 1976 Inflation is up 71
percent." Usually we are more conscious of the
crunch than we are of the cushion. According to
the above figures, for those who earn salaries,
Income has more than compensated for Inflation.
During this same ten-year period our church
budget went up by only 61 percent. Obviously,

we have operated our church program with honest frugality while within that same period we substantially increased our mission giving.

Raymond B. Knudsen in "New Models for Creative Giving" writes that when it comes to charitable giving we simply have not advanced with the times. This does not mean that we are not giving more than when a postcard was a penny and a cup of coffee was a thin dime. It does mean, however, that pledges have not kept pace with escalation.

Giving is an expression of spiritual commitment. What little or large increase we may make in our pledge for 19_ can make a difference, beginning here at home and reaching out to the world. This lovely prayer by Jill Schaeffer can stimulate our creativity as we think about our pledges for the new year.

"I am a materialist, Lord. So, I offer this money as a symbol of my deep humility. Take it then, from this servant who knows no other gift that can bridge distances, raise buildings, feed the hungry and heal the sick, going places where I cannot go, helping people whom I will never meet. Take this money, knowing my poor understanding of this world and its sorrow, my honest attempts to do that which I can do, and give that which I can give. Take this money for what it is: a means to Your ends. And take also, the imagination of Your Church that tries to realize Your Kingdom through the use of money. Take it and the hope that goes with it as you would our faith and love, and we pray that it is used wisely, beautifully, and faithfully, to increase Your Glory. In Jesus' name. Amen."

As mentioned elsewhere, a yearly theme adds interest and freshness to the annual canvass period. For instance, "Count me, therefore, a partner" (Philemon 1:17)—KJV) can be the title of a sermon, the theme on the letterhead, pledge

card, envelopes, packets and the closing line of
all interpretive material. By the same token, a
sustained emphasis can be used over a period of
several years. This was documented in a fine
article: "The First Step—One to Forty," by Wil-
burn O. Budd, Financial Secretary of the First
Presbyterian Church of Amarillo, Texas. It
appeared in the November 1965 issue of *Church
Management.*

His thesis is that a person giving only 2 or 3
percent of income, but wanting to tithe, has a
very difficult mental and practical jump from 2
percent one year to 5 or 10 percent the next.
Because of the large hurdle, many individuals
simply continue giving a fixed amount. The giant
step frightens them. However, with a concerted
effort over several years encouraging a step-up in
proportion, individuals can move from a small
percentage to the desired goal. Mr. Budd
divided the giving of his church into dollar units
showing how much of the total yearly budget
was contributed by those within a given category. The canvass committee then began an active campaign to move everybody up one step
into a new giving division each year. They used
the words of their pastor, Dr. James R. Carroll, as
incentive: "If each member would take 'one
step-up,' the Church could probably take ten
steps forward."

Such a sustained theme has positive results, as
Mr. Budd points out in his article. This author's
experience also verifies that fact. The "step-up"
wording and emphasis can be done with small
letters and caps in printing or typing. Give con-

tinued visibility to the theme whenever possible: step By STEP. This positive message has helped many individuals move up the pledge ladder from nominal contributer to tither. Not only is the church of Jesus Christ stimulated to further mission by such growth, but the person who experiences this kind of maturity also finds an incredible joy in what previously had been merely routine.

Martin Luther once said that there were two kinds of conversion: conversion of the heart and conversion of the pocketbook. The art of canvass contributes to both.

· 15 ·

THE YOUTH BUDGET

EVERY church must recognize the importance
of educating children and youth in stewardship.
Through the youth budget program, young
people accept a certain percentage or amount of
the total congregational budget as their
responsibility. All church school young people
are invited to pledge. Special offering envelopes
are issued and quarterly accounts mailed to each
participant. Such a program is invaluable as a
teaching and training experience. It also gives
the congregation an awareness of youth involvement. Many learn the meaning of tithing while
participating in the youth budget. The experience marks them for life. Young people today are handling increasingly larger amounts of
money because of better paying part-time jobs or
more generous allowances. Given a chance to
shape their own priorities, they are often far
more visionary in their generosity than adults. It
is not unusual to have youth-budget-trained
youth pledging and giving $2.00 to $5.00 per
week during their later high school or community college years. The church is responsible

for nurturing these future members in the meaning of stewardship.

If a particular congregation appoints committees annually, the youth budget committee should be included. This gives recognition to the importance of young people in the life of their church and visibility to their involvement. Those serving should be related to the youth organizational structure, with junior high and senior high representatives. A youth budget chairperson is then elected, usually a high school senior who has had previous experience on the committee. An adult advisor can be appointed by the canvass chairperson or selected by the minister. Where there is a staff, one person should be assigned to work with the group.

The initial meeting is held in early fall to plan, set a theme and establish a realistic budget quota. The quota usually has two parts so that the proportion of General Mission (benevolence) to Local Mission (current expenses) can be emphasized. If a $1,500 goal is established, it might be divided on a two-to-one basis: $1,000 for Local Mission and $500 for General Mission. Plans must also be initiated for the type of promotion and presentation that will be given to the church school classes and youth groups. Details of the youth canvass are discussed and dates established. A common practice is to hold youth Loyalty Sunday on the same day as adult Loyalty Sunday. All junior high and senior high youth who have not pledged by that morning are visited by their peers in the afternoon. Children from three years of age through sixth grade are invited to pledge, with parents signing the card. Seventh graders and above are asked to sign their own pledges.

Presentations to the church school department can be as imaginative as the talents of the committee. Members of the Youth Budget Cabinet often write and produce their own material, following the theme of the current canvass. They use slides, films, puppets, skits and dialogue. These ten- or fifteen-minute presentations should be scheduled over a period of two or three Sundays so that every classroom can be visited. Posters by young artists are placed around the church building for emphasis.

Teachers and church school personnel should be briefed on the meaning of youth stewardship at the fall teachers' meeting. Devote a portion of time to the importance of stewardship training and how the teacher can complement classroom presentations. Initial plans include a suitable dedication of pledges in every department or classroom. Coordination is essential for a unified emphasis on the importance of stewardship.

Teachers are again reminded by letter:

Dear Teacher:

You have a unique opportunity to interpret and explain the youth stewardship and mission emphasis to the children of our church school.

1. YOUTH STEWARDSHIP trains young people in systematic and proportionate giving (I Corinthians 16:1-3) and informs them how their money is used in the church's total mission.

2. YOUTH STEWARDSHIP ENROLLMENT SUNDAY is November 8 (Loyalty

The Youth Budget

Sunday). Children and youth will be asked to bring their Youth Budget Pledge Cards at that time. We ask that EACH CHURCH SCHOOL CLASS have a special pledge dedication.

3. Everyone from pre-school (age three) through high school may enroll. Parents of pre-school through sixth graders are asked to sign pledges for their children. Junior high and older will be asked to sign their own pledges.

4. All children and youth will receive offering envelopes before January 1, 19_. A record of contribution is maintained only for those who pledge.

There will be stewardship presentations in all the classrooms. (See attached schedule.)

If there are any questions about the program please contact me. Thank you for your help.

Sincerely

Linda K. Smith, Chairperson
Youth Budget Committee

Information about the Youth Budget regularly appears in the church bulletin and newsletter, so all parents are generally informed. Late in October they are encouraged, by mail, to interpret youth stewardship to their children.

Dear Parent:

We hope that through the following information you and your child will better understand youth stewardship and become personally involved in our church's mission.

THE PURPOSE OF YOUTH STEWARDSHIP

... To teach our children and youth to take their part in the work of Christ's church, here at home and throughout the world.

95

... To teach our young people a systematic method of returning to God a definite portion of the many gifts we have received from him (I Cor. 16:1–3).

WHO TAKES PART IN THIS PLAN?

... Any child or young person in our church from age three through high school may make a pledge. We hope that everyone will pledge for 19—.

HOW DOES ONE MAKE A PLEDGE?

... Pledge cards and special youth stewardship material will be sent in a later mailing. Fill out the pledge card and return on Loyalty Sunday, November 8.

... Children or youth who cannot attend that day are asked to mail their pledges before November 8.

We appreciate your interest and pray that we may do our part in the mission of Christ's Church.

Sincerely,

Linda K. Smith, Chairperson
Youth Budget Committee

THE YOUTH BUDGET FOR 19— IS $1,500, WITH $1,000 TO BE USED FOR LOCAL MISSION AND $500 FOR GENERAL MISSION

Approximately a week later, the second letter is sent to parents of children ages three through sixth grade. Pledge cards are included for all children in the household sixth grade and younger. The parent is asked to sign the card but to discuss the matter with the child.

Dear Parent:

You recently received a letter concerning our youth stewardship and Loyalty Sunday program. Enclosed you will find additional items to help you in explaining youth stewardship to your child.

The Youth Budget

Our theme this year is: "Keep Our Tree Growing." The tree represents the church and the water is money contributed. We feel that children can easily understand the concept of watering a tree.

We want them to understand that their contributions are important and helpful. We also want them to realize that as the tree grows and reaches out, so the church extends itself through mission. Their support is vital to growth.

Thank you for your cooperation. Please remember to have your child return the pledge on Loyalty Sunday, November 8, with one of your signatures on it. If it is not possible to be present that day, please mail the card.

Sincerely yours,

Linda K. Smith, Chairperson
Youth Budget Committee

On the day the above letter is sent to parents of children, a personal note from the Youth Budget Chairperson is mailed to all junior and senior high youth, seventh through twelfth graders. It is written by a peer and speaks their language. Youth in this age category are asked to sign their own pledge cards and return on Loyalty Sunday. Those who do not return them on that day are visited by youth canvassers.

Hi!

This year the Youth Budget Committee has decided to use "Keep Our Tree Growing" as the theme for pledging. Our Church is involved in helping people locally, nationally and world wide. We, the youth, can help that growth by increasing our pledges. Just as a tree needs water, the church needs your pledge. If you could raise it just a nickel or dime, it would be greatly appreciated.

97

We would also like to have you come down to
grow with us in our youth fellowship.
Your friend,

Linda K. Smith, Chairperson
Youth Budget Committee

· 16 ·

YOUTH CANVASS ARRANGEMENTS

AT LEAST three weeks before the second Sunday of November, young people in the youth groups are invited to serve as visitors for the canvass. An explanation can be given at the regular weekly fellowship, with a sign-up sheet available. Members of the youth committee may need to telephone additional people insuring adequate personnel for the anticipated number of calls. Senior high youth who can drive are asked to indicate the availability of a car for that day. Additional drivers may be secured from adults who cannot canvass on the first Sunday in November but would be available to chauffeur youth visitors on the second Sunday.

ORGANIZING FOR VISITATION

Duplicate 3 x 5 cards are prepared with the name, address and parish zone number of each junior and senior high youth. On Loyalty Sunday a core group of young people and adults should be at the operations center, where they can work fast without interruption. As the youth pledge cards are brought in following church school, they are immediately separated (cards should have a place to indicate age and grade). Those sixth grade and under are placed in one grouping. Seventh through twelfth grades are placed in another group and immediately alphabetized. For every pledge received, both 3 x 5 cards are removed and placed in a "no call" box. When the process is completed, remaining cards represent individuals who have not pledged. One set of 3 x 5 cards is left in the master file. The other set is removed and calls are quickly arranged by geographical zone, with five or six cards per team. Teams of two have already been designated from the volunteer list. Calls assigned to each team are jotted down on a half-sheet, with the visitors' names at the top.

TRAINING

The youth callers gather for lunch on Loyalty Sunday. While they are eating, calls are being organized. Adult drivers are invited to eat with the youth visitors and have been notified of meal and assignment. Youth callers have also been reminded of their assignment by note. Following the meal, the adult advisor, minister and youth chairperson make a three-part presentation:

1. The meaning, purpose and necessity of youth budget.
2. How to make a call, handle indifference, hostility, youth, parents, etc., and what to say on the call.
3. The mechanics of the canvass (writing comments on 3 x 5 cards, material to be left at homes and reporting back).

After the training session, teams and drivers are announced and given time to meet each other. Good balance and training result in pairing a junior high youth with a senior high youth and mixing sexes. High school people driving their own cars should be given a partner known to be reliable and mature. Adults who drive do not assist with calls. This is a youth responsibility.

MATERIAL

In addition to their lists, the callers carry with them helpful interpretive material. This includes mimeographed information about the church school, events and activities of the youth fellowship, choir schedule, and something about the mission enterprise of the church. Extra pledge cards are also provided.

REPORTING-IN

The adult advisor and a member of the staff need to be on hand to receive all callers. Many will return with pledges. Others have notes on their 3 x 5 cards they wish to discuss. This provides another channel for keeping in touch with and obtaining information about the parish. Pledge cards are brought to the office for inclusion in Loyalty Sunday totals. Those turned in during the morning service have already been alphabetized by core committee members and pledges figured on a yearly basis.

FOLLOW-UP

Within two weeks after Loyalty Sunday, a follow-up letter should be mailed to those who have not pledged. Young people who are members of the church receive a specific letter addressed to them concerning their membership commitment with regard to church support.

• 17 •

STEWARDSHIP SERMONS

"IN A VERY real sense every sermon is a stewardship sermon, for it must always be undergirded with the recognition of God's sovereignty and man's responsibility. The sovereignty of God extends over every aspect of man's life, including his pocketbook, and stewardship concerns not only money but man's whole existence in responsibility to God." (Kantonen, *Select Stewardship Sermons*, Foreword) The subject needs to be specifically discussed, practically and theologically, as the people prepare to make their pledges. The sermon "On The First Day of The Week" was preached on Visitation Sunday. "The Peril of No Perspective" is an example of a Loyalty Sunday sermon, as is "On Keeping Commitments."

ON THE FIRST DAY OF THE WEEK

Saturday night was always important in the home of my childhood. I can still recall the scene vividly—its lesson and imprint remains to this day. After the dinner dishes had been cleared, my father, of sainted memory, would sit at the dining room table and take from his pocket an envelope which contained his earnings for the week. This was a solemn occasion. There were times when that little envelope seemed quite inadequate for the responsibility it must bear.

These were depression years, when even copper coins were terribly precious. My father had labored long and lovingly for the contents of that little envelope. It represented some sixty hours of hard work at his small store, not counting additional hours of bookkeeping and letter writing at home.

The moment of attainment had now arrived. Reaching inside, he withdrew the contents: thirty-three dollars in one dollar bills and coins. A modest, yet adequate, sum for those traumatic times. And while I gazed fondly on that accumulation of this world's goods, which on occasions I was permitted to do, another drama took place before my very eyes.

This was the act of thanksgiving, worship and high devotion. Very carefully my father first took three dollars and thirty cents and placed it in another envelope marked "church." That money was his tithe, and it was sacred. It was never touched but for its intended use—to be presented in the house of the Lord on the first day of the week. It always came off the top. Everything else was secondary.

Then followed the ritual of placing coins and bills in other envelopes—for mortgage payments, food, clothing and other necessities of life. At times it was a long and painful process, moments of solemn deliberation and concentrated thought, to make each coin stretch to its full value. But there was never any question about what came first and what was foremost.

As I recall that scene in my mind's eye, the words of St. Paul come echoing across the years: "Now concerning the collection ... Upon the first day of the week let every one of you lay by him in store, as God hath prospered him ..." (I Corinthians 16:1a and 2b—KJV). There is a definite relationship between money and religion.

We cannot separate the two, much as we try at times. The teaching of stewardship principles is a primary task and duty of the church. A church that fails to teach about and talk about stewardship is as guilty of dereliction in duty as the church that fails to talk about the cross of Christ during Holy Week.

For the cross is the highest expression of stewardship. And if we believe the message of the cross, we also must be equally concerned about the mission of the cross, which channels itself through the church. We are stewards of the message. The giving of money for Christ and his church, when properly motivated, is a completely valid form of personal witness to one's faith. Not only is it a valid witness, it is a vital and necessary witness.

Jesus used every opportunity to instruct people in the right use of the things they possessed. To him, the most serious problem standing in the way of a man's complete relationship with God, was the matter of possessions. He understood that the most sensitive nerve in

104

many a person's body is his pocketbook. Someone has calculated that one sixth of Jesus' recorded teachings are concerned with the matter of possessions. One third of all his parables are devoted to that subject.

I am told that there are about five hundred references to prayer in the Bible, about five hundred references to faith, but more than one thousand to a man and his possessions. Now, if there are one thousand references in the Bible to a man and his possessions, then it must be an important and vital subject. This need not surprise us. Religion is life—all of life. You cannot separate the two. And since life is, necessarily, much concerned with money, religion must have something to say about it. It does!

Every thoughtful Christian knows that he owes his life and breath and measure of happiness to the Maker. But it remains too often an abstraction; it is not always a stimulating awareness. It does not strike home to him as tangibly as the bills in his mail. Yet, we are all wards of divine charity.

Starting with the book of Genesis we read: "In the beginning God created . . ." The Psalmist picks up the refrain and chants, "It is he that hath made us, and not we ourselves." Again, the Psalmist, emphasizing the majesty of God and man's indebtedness, writes: "The earth is the Lord's and the fulness thereof; the world and they that dwell therein." When one is logical and honest, there is recognition that all he possesses comes from the giver of "every good and perfect gift."

But let us not stop our thinking merely with tangible gifts given us by a loving creator: the bounty of harvest, the beauty of sunset, the miracle of natural resources and life itself. Moving into the New Testament we cannot escape the insistent reality and meaning of the gift of Christmas and the gift of Easter. Perhaps we need to ask ourselves again and again, "Why?" And who can miss the meaning of "why" in that keystone verse of our faith: "For God so loved the world that he gave his only Son, that whoever believes in him should not perish but have eternal life" (John 3:16—RSV). God gave, not counting the cost, because he so loved.

When I think about the sacrifice of Christ as the supreme fact of history, then the poet's words have a very personal meaning:

> Ah, when I look up at the Cross
> Where God's great Steward suffered loss
> Of life, and shed His blood for me,
> A trifling thing it seems to be,
> To give a gift, dear Lord, to Thee,
> Of time or talent, wealth or store . . .
> Full well I know I owe Thee more;
> A million times I owe Thee more!
>
> (author unknown)

When we talk about Christian stewardship we are really talking about our faith. As church members we have accepted God's offer of salvation in Jesus Christ. He has made it possible and we have responded to his offer. Our response is a matter of faith. One of the things that Jesus taught about faith is that it is not a self-contained thing. We are not to hoard our faith like the miser nor bury it in the ground like the unfortunate steward. Our Lord said that we are to be witnesses: teaching, preaching, baptizing, proclaiming and demonstrating. He said that we are to feed his sheep: go, do and serve. This is faith in action, and the only kind of real faith there is.

Since Jesus founded the church to preserve and proclaim the gospel, it is natural and necessary that the Christian will channel his faith actively through the church. "Let your light so shine before men that they may see your good works and give glory to your Father who is in heaven" (Matthew 5:16—RSV). Much of what the church is able to accomplish in the world is made possible only through financial stewardship.

Stewardship is partnership—our partnership with God, our involvement with his enterprises—the active response of our faith to his love. When a person exchanges part of his life for money, he has an opportunity to reinvest that time and money in the mission of Christ by contributing money through the church. When we give money, we give ourselves. There is a vast difference between giving and paying. Paying is part of an obligation we have incurred. Giving is a voluntary response to what one believes. It is his faith in action. If one believes little he gives little. If one believes deeply he gives generously and sacrificially. We can think that one over a long time and its ultimate reality is still the same.

A Christian bears witness to his faith in many ways, not the least of which is expressing that faith through money. The idea that talking about money from the pulpit has no place in Christian worship is one of the most specious bits of reasoning that has ever intimidated the full proclamation of the gospel of Jesus Christ. It is sheer rationalization of the greatest magnitude. A minister who fails to talk about the Christian concept of money, responsible discipleship and the spiritual implications of stewardship stands guilty of not preaching the full gospel. The church has been entrusted with the Good News by Jesus Christ, to be preserved and passed along. The church, therefore, cannot remain static. It must become a dynamic fellowship existing for the gospel it proclaims and for all people everywhere. Its mandate is not to be exclusive, clutching the precious gospel to itself. Rather, it is to be inclusive, reaching out in love with the good news of redemption.

Next Sunday is Loyalty Sunday in First Church. It can be a day of monumental significance or a day of unattempted valor, depending on our attitude, outlook and personal commitment to the cause of Christ. David A. Redding says it this way: "But the question remains: 'What will I give to God for the next year?' His business cannot run on the piggy banks of camp followers. It stands or falls on the stewardship of the people, not on the surplus of leftovers. We pick out our gifts for friends very carefully. We certainly don't ordinarily make it a practice to give them the same this year we gave last year, except under unusual circumstances.

Unavoidably, the value of our gift conveys the extent of our affection. God can't help drawing conclusions if our Christmas shopping bill exceeds his gift" (Redding, *Presbyterian Life*, 15 October 1962).

I can think of no better words than those of Paul to take home and ponder for the week: "Now concerning the collection ... Upon the first day of the week let every one of you lay by him in store, as God hath prospered him." Paul was not talking amounts. He was talking percentages. He was saying to those members of the First Church of Corinth that God prospers people on various levels. To some he may have given more abilities or talents than to others. Nevertheless, as he has prospered, so we are to express gratitude. This is proportionate giving, which means that all gifts are made equal, not in terms of amount, but in terms of percentage of prosperity.

Voluntarily then, through percentage giving we are able to express the full intent of our concern and love, based on a realistic scale which takes into consideration either increases or decreases in the state of our affairs. That is being honest with God. That is all he asks.

This is theology in its most expressive form. Or, as Paul says in a second letter to his fellow Christians in Corinth, "Moreover, your very giving proves the reality of your faith, and that means that men thank God that you practise the gospel that you profess to believe in, as well as for the actual gifts you make to them and to others" (II Corinthians 9:13—J.B. Phillips). They are inseparably bound. Faith and works now become one in the sight of God.

THE PERIL OF NO PERSPECTIVE

"And Peter said to Jesus, 'Lord it is well that we are here; if you wish, I will make three booths here, one for you and one for Moses and one for Elijah.' "

(Matthew 17:4—RSV)

All of us, I am certain, have been intrigued by the imaginative tale of Rip Van Winkle. He sought out a nice quiet spot on the banks of the Hudson River and went to sleep for some twenty years. The day he entered into his long siesta, the sign over his favorite inn was George III. He was a subject of the British crown. When he awakened the sign was George Washington. He was an American citizen.

But the tragic part of the interesting tale is that he slept through a momentous revolution. While he snored, oblivious to his surroundings, fantastic events were taking place. Men were shaping the destiny of a mighty nation with sacrifices written in blood ... offering their lives, their fortunes and their sacred honor as a down payment on their future. While he blissfully slumbered, men of perspective were writing a Declaration of Independence and forging a Constitution that birthed a society of the free.

Escaping from reality, he withheld a part of himself from one of the greatest enterprises in human history: the establishment of a unique society that was waiting to be born. He was outside the sphere of action that was taking place. It is a common temptation to find such allurement and contentment with the present that it precludes any vision of duty, danger or daring.

In our Scripture Lesson from the seventeenth chapter of Matthew we read about the Transfiguration of Christ. Jesus took Peter, James and John with him and they went up into a high mountain. While they were there, Jesus was transfigured before them ... his face shone like the sun and his garments became white as light ... and there appeared to them Moses and Elijah. This phenomenon is hard to visualize and understand. Quite obviously, it was a supernatural occurrence.

Why did it happen? It has been interpreted that this mystical experience was God's signature on Christ's commitment to the course he must follow. Our Lord had a perspective about the outcome of his life that was not a pleasant prospect. In the chapter prior to the transfiguration story, we find him telling his disciples that the close of his ministry would eventuate in a cross. There was a path of lowliness and sorrow ahead that needed to be followed, unpleasant though it might appear. In the midst of his own conflicting emotions there came this strange interlude of enlightenment and the very same voice that had commissioned him at baptism spoke out of the clouds saying, "This is my beloved Son, in whom I am well pleased, hear ye him."

In that moment Jesus knew once again that eternal life is round about well-chosen death, that apparent failure can be truest gain, and that the Father was pleased in the commitment of the Son. In this profound encounter he was transformed and renewed. He was blessed to become a further blessing to all mankind, even though his journey was to take him through the valley of the shadow of death. The vision that he received as his responsibility was re-confirmed with God's stamp of approval and he was strengthened for his task. Truly this was an unforgettable mountaintop experience.

The three disciples were eye witnesses to what happened. Overcome by the intensity of the experience, Peter could not contain himself. "Lord," he said, "How good it is that we are here. If you like, I will make three booths here, one for you and one for Moses and one for Elijah." The three booths or tents would be used as places of retirement and worship for the three principals in the drama. Overcome by the moment or deliberately choosing not to hear Peter, our Lord made no answer to the offer. Peter was trying to say, "What a tremendous experience. Let's try to keep it alive by staying here and dwelling on its majesty. Let's remain in this place, Lord, and never go back to the crowds, the concerns, the caprices of mortal men, and the cross. Let's stay forever and never break the spell." It was an eloquent silence that answered his offer.

Soon thereafter, they were journeying down the mountain to involvement. Christ's task on earth was not completed and he knew it. There was to be no staying, longing after a quivering moment of surpassing beauty. The peril of no perspective would have left our Lord seated in bliss atop a mountain rather than lifted high on a cross drawing all men unto him. The first might have been more desirable and comfortable. But the second brought about the salvation of the world. Perspective made the difference. Christ could not stay isolated, untouched by the tides and currents of an eventful life that sought as its highest aim to do the Father's will and leave a legacy of love broad enough and deep enough for the needs of all mankind.

If Christ had stayed as Peter suggested there would have been no cross, no church and no Christianity. He could not stay nor would he stay. The pull of perspective brought him down from the mountain with renewed determination to follow the gleam. On the other hand, there have been some who felt they had descended so low in the valley of sin, despair or frustration that they wanted to stay put, simply because they had lost the vision and given up. The same Elijah who appeared on the mountain as a saint was at one time a defeated man in the valley of despair. He had an unsuccessful encounter with the evil King Ahab and his wicked wife Jezebel. He felt a failure. Going into the wilderness, he sat under a juniper tree and asked that he might die. He wanted to stay right there and let the end come. There are people who feel like that. Their burdens seem more than they can bear. They want to lie down some place, wrap themselves in misery and throw away the key.

A loss of perspective can do that to a person. But God laid a hand on Elijah, gave him a vision of something significant and he found he no longer wanted to stay put. He wanted to do something creative with his life. But for a good many the message never gets through. Nothing counters their resignation and melancholy. They want to curl up and hibernate. So they say, "I'll just stay right here with my broken hopes and broken heart and put in my time. . . . I don't care enough any more to even try." And so they exist, atrophy, wither, die. Skid row is filled with many a man who has accepted himself for his worst. Convinced he can become no better, bereft of all hope, he says, "I'll just stay here."

But skid row is not the only place. There are defeated souls who sit and brood away their time in respectable surroundings, utterly convinced that they are worthless, useless, meaningless and that life has no purpose. Having lost the vision and finding themselves at dead end, they say, "This is it. Here I'll remain content with my misery."

Others reach a plateau in their thinking. In 1838 a man resigned from the United States Patent Office because, he said in his letter of resignation, "there is no future in the Patent Office; all the great inventions have been accomplished." Since that myopic man resigned, we have discovered the steam engine, the diesel engine, the jet propulsion engine, the telephone, television, radio, autos, airships, miracle drugs, atomic power and space craft, to name but a few. Content with the splendor of the gas era, he wrapped up his mind in a nice neat package and blissfully walked off into oblivion. Many a

114

business, industry or institution has died a premature death, content with its own self image. Lacking desire, concern, initiative, vision; satisfied with what seemed to be the ultimate, they perished because they wanted to stay put. There is no growth in a vacuum.

Only where progress prevails and where perspective is unlimited is the good made better, the last achievement used as the foundation for the next accomplishment and the future becomes complete with the promise of yesterday. No man knows all the answers. When he thinks he does, then he has died mentally. He's fenced himself off from the reality of new questions, content with his little knowledge, finding false security in his authoritarianism. The person who says, "I don't want to grow any more, I just want to stay here," is misusing the capacity for intelligence which God has given him. The mind cannot wear out. But it cannot be put out to pasture either.

In a New England Academy, the dynamic young headmaster, faced with the task of selecting a department head, ignored seniority and appointed a younger man. After the announcement, a disgruntled member of the department came to him with indignation, demanding to know why his twenty years' experience had been overlooked. "My friend," said the courageous headmaster, "In reality, you haven't had twenty years' experience. You've had one year's experience twenty times." The peril of no perspective is to live with a closed mind, year after year after year, *ad infinitum.*

It affects not only the mental attitude, but any spiritual aspiration as well. There are some who confuse the simplicity of Christ's teachings and way of life with a fixed, stereotyped kind of piety. A static, rigid, sterile, uncreative spiritual life is in effect saying, "This is good. . . . I'll not complicate it with any growth that might disturb the status quo. I'll stay right here and close my eyes, ears and heart to such threats as the social gospel, the church in mission, personal involvement and new forms or ways of ministry, witness and worship. Being narrowly bound in on all sides is to feel smug and safe and secure. To stay here means to oppose change, growth, development which might unseat a small sense of well-being with things as they are."

There is such a thing as a Church occupying itself with the forms and ceremonies of religion and leaving Christ out, side-stepping live questions, straddling theological and controversial issues, fleeing to the safety zone of fervent reiteration of pious platitudes, merely maintaining ecclesiastical machinery and shrinking from the dangerous business of adventuresome Christian living. Jesus called the churchmen of his day, the Pharisees, "dead men." What he meant was that they had arrived at a certain place in their spiritual habits and here they planned to stay. In the eyes of Jesus, they were dead because they would not grow. They had no perspective, only a small and sanctified contentment.

A favorite cartoon of mine shows a well-dressed and overfed dowager leaving church on

Sunday, shaking hands with the parson at the door and saying, "Wonderful sermon . . . everything you said applies to somebody or other I know." A spiritually small but eminently satisfied soul.

One of the most exciting stories in the Bible is the call of God to Abraham, already old and having known more than his share of the struggle of life. When he was ninety years old, God appeared to him and said, "I will make of you a great nation." Almost a century of life and God comes to him with a new concept. "And Abraham went out, not knowing where he went." Following the direction of the Almighty, this great saint allowed nothing to obscure his perspective. At his advanced age it would have been easy to say to God: "Let some younger man do it . . . let another have the responsibility. I've had so much living, I'd just like to settle down with my flock and my family and taper off a bit. I'm not your man, Lord, I just want to stay here." By faith Abraham went where God led. No staying put for him!

Let me say one final thing. The peril of no perspective can affect the heart as well. Our Lord could not really have shown his love for mankind by hiding out on a mountain. By staying there, as Peter suggested, he could never have taken the sacrificial cross and made of it a symbol of salvation and love's highest devotion.

Something like this confronts our Christian stewardship today. When we take stock of the program of our local church, our denominational activity in this country and throughout the world, we can take some satisfaction in the accomplishments that have been and are being made. To have them fully in focus is an awe-inspiring experience.

It's an amazing thing what God has done with the generosity of Christians both past and present. How easy to live in the glow of great accomplishments, forgetting that the mystical multiplication comes as the loaves and fishes are blessed. It is God Himself who takes what we share and makes it effective far beyond its normal and mortal capacity. The temptation comes to take pride in our accomplishments, rather than seeing the more that needs to be done. Not only must we maintain, but fully as important, we must enlarge! Churches or individuals staying static in their love, loyalty and generosity are churches and individuals in retreat. There is no neutrality. Either we go forward or we regress.

"It is good that we are here," said Peter to Jesus. It was greeted with silence. "Let us build shrines and stay in this place," said Peter. Again no answer. But we do read that they came down the mountain. Not words but action. Our Lord had no idea of maintaining a vigil on a plateau. He meant to enlarge the work he had been commissioned to do, and that he did . . . completing it at the price of his own life on a cross.

To maintain and enlarge . . . at a price! This is our stewardship challenge. There is a relationship between our growth in the faith and our faithfulness as stewards. The man who year after year says, "make mine the same," when he is capable of more, is really building a shrine of contentment and saying, "I think I've done enough ... I'll just stay here." He's closed his mind, his soul, his heart to the continued blessings of God's love and generosity.

But God cannot build out of such limited love. It takes courage to look at the cross. The cross is God's way of saying, "I could not stay content until I had done everything in my power to redeem mankind." It's Christ's way of saying, "Love never ends when it has the longer view, for the long view has no limits." Therefore, the cross tells me that God does not hold himself back with the satisfaction that he has done enough, until he has done everything on my behalf.

My stewardship then becomes the real expression of how much I understand the meaning of the cross. I need an open heart, mind and soul to comprehend. My stewardship is my humility, my gratitude, my vision of who I am, who God is, and what he wants me to do in and for his world. "It's good that we are here," but we can't stay "here" forever. There is work to be done at home and abroad. Some we can do by our expression of faith in society. It means our time and talents and witness. But that is not all. What we leave of ourselves, through our gifts of love, God sends forth with mighty energy and superior power to minister on our behalf in his name.

To maintain and enlarge ... this is our call, our challenge, our task and our love laid bare in partnership with God for the redemption of the

world. Says the book of Proverbs: "Where there
is no vision, the people perish." We have not arrived. We are not content with staying here. We
are always in the process of arriving until one
day there comes that call serene and clear: "Well
done, good and faithful steward, enter into the
joy of thy reward."

ON KEEPING COMMITMENTS

". . . And he answered and said, I go, sir: and
went not."

(Matthew 21:30b—KJV)

A father once said to his son: "Go and work in
the vineyard today. The harvest is great. We are
short of help. The crop must be saved. It is ur-
gent that every member of the household do his
part." There was good reason for this simple request: "go and work in the vineyard today." And
the son answered, "I go, sir."

What the father asked, the son responded to
with a verbal affirmation. The same request had
been rudely denied by his brother. The brother
wanted no part of a commitment that would in-
volve his time or energy in such enterprise. Let
the grapes rot. He was a free spirit, with a mind
of his own. He would do as he pleased.

When the father heard the second son say, "I
go, sir," he breathed a sigh of relief. Here, at
least, was someone in his family who was
sensitive to need and responsive to the situation
without regard to personal preferences. Here
was a man after his own heart who respected
authority, faced reality honestly, assumed
responsibility and had the grace to respond

120

promptly without question or lip service.

But, the narrative account of this brief parable of our Lord takes a strange turn. ". . . And he answered and said, I go, sir: and went not" (Matthew 21:30b—KJV). The story is utterly direct and to the point. "I go, sir: and went not," is in six words a description of an age-old problem and one of life's serious sins.

The broken promise, the unkept commitment, the unfulfilled vow can be as serious a sin as the most heinous crime. Clayton Barbeau, writing in his new book, *Creative Marriage: The Middle Years*, says, "Many people don't fool around but are completely unfaithful to their marital commitment of love, the commitment to help one another grow. It's even more grievous to neglect that responsibility than to indulge in extramarital sex."

The poet puts it in another way:

> I never cut my neighbor's throat
> My neighbor's purse I never stole;
> I never spoiled his house and land,
> But God have mercy on my soul.
> For I am haunted night and day
> By all the deeds I have not done,
> That unattempted loveliness,
> Oh, costly valor, never won.
>
> *Guilty*,
> by Marguerite Wilkinson)

The son in the story did not keep his word. He did not fulfill his commitment. He made a promise and failed to follow through. Mentally he affirmed something that morally he did not bring to a conclusion. Perhaps he was a dishonest person. There are those who say they will do something with no real intent of holding themselves to what they said they would do. This is a sophisticated form of lying.

People make promises to resist pressure. They know they are not telling the truth. "I'll take care of it tomorrow." But tomorrow never comes. They deliberately deceive others: family, friends, customers, clients and even God. They deceive themselves as well. In short, they bear false witness. And this is one of the destroying qualities that despoils life and the relationships of life. Yet, the capacity to have relationships with other human beings is one of God's greatest gifts to mankind.

The son may have calmly looked his father in the eye, responded yes, and in his heart he knew all the time he would not carry out his commitment. Has not many an anguished parent wept into the silences of the night over such deceit? And then I think of God who reads the mind of man and the anguish he must bear, of promises not intended—many made in his name.

On the other hand, the son may have had every good intention of doing his father's bidding. He may have set out deliberately to fulfill his obligation. Yet, somewhere between his intention and his destination, something changed his course of action. Some allurement intruded on his determination. Perhaps it was such a nice day that he decided to go fishing instead. Whatever it was, something came between his commitment and the confirmation of it. He broke his word.

This becomes then a matter of integrity, of personal character and trustworthiness. A commitment is never a casual thing. It is a self-promise and therefore indicates one's authenticity as a person. Or it is a personal vow made to God as an act of responsibility such as in baptismal, marriage or church membership vows. The true test of life's demands and the mark of one's morality expresses itself not in what one's answer is, but in what one's actions are.

There are few in this life who have escaped the frustration of a broken promise. How we are hurt, angered, humiliated and embarrassed by those who respect themselves so little that they are not as good as their word, who fail to keep their commitments. Every life has been touched by broken promises.

Yet, we have not always learned from our own hurt. For by the same token, we too have contributed to the world's misery by our own lack of fidelity to an indication of intent. And I think of God, who has been hurt beyond measure by unkept commitments, broken promises and deedless words. Yet, he is still the same: yesterday, today and forever—for he cannot deny himself.

When Solomon dedicated the temple he noted this and said, "Blessed be the Lord who has given rest to his people Israel, according to all that he promised; not one word has failed of all his good promises, which he uttered by Moses his servant" (I Kings 8:56—RSV). The entire Bible is a book of God's promises to man, which he keeps. Almighty God, who is as good as his word, who keeps his commitments, has established standards which he expects of his children.

But not only does this story have to do with personal conduct on the day-to-day level. It has future implications as well. It was told to the good church people of Christ's day, the Pharisees and their followers. Jesus told the parable and said, in conclusion: "The Publicans and harlots go into the kingdom of God before you." This was, to say the least, shocking language to be directed at the nice people of that age. The worst people you can think of will enter the kingdom before you will, no matter how good you think you are. There is a sense of urgency here for every generation. He is saying in essence: "You are insincere, for you make a pretense of honoring God and then fail utterly in the rest of your deeds." Commitment is an expression of faith—convictions expressed in action.

"Wherewith shall I come before Jehovah, and bow myself before the high God?" they asked of an old prophet. "With burnt offerings?" "No," he answered, "you cannot ceremonialize your way into God's favor." "With thousands of rams?" "No, you cannot bribe the Eternal." "With ten thousands of oil?" "No, you cannot ease yourself into the Divine presence." "Then I will give my first-born for my transgressions, the fruit of my body for the sin of my soul." "No!" thundered the old prophet, "you cannot seduce God even with shed blood! He hath showed thee, O man, what is good; and what doth Jehovah require of thee, but to do justly, and to love kindness, and to walk humbly with thy God?" So one shows the presence of God in daily life not only by the faith he feels, but by the commitments he keeps. For commitments are the sacred enactment of the values one holds.

This is what Jesus is trying to emphasize. He warns in his parable that emotion which says, "I go," and is not straightway translated into deeds is an insincerity even worse than curt denial. To affirm something in the mind and with the voice is reality only when there is a corresponding response.

The Christian life is a series of commitments, vows made to God which become valid when demonstrated in daily life. Parents who present their children for baptism, promise with the help of God that they will bring up their children in the nurture and admonition of the Lord. This is a life-long commitment to love them, be concerned for their spiritual welfare and be a worthy example to them. This is not always easy, as parents well know. The words are the declaration of intent. The rest of one's life is spent in carrying them out. Many times parents remind their children of the fifth commandment: "Honor thy father and thy mother." On occasions it becomes necessary for children to remind their parents of the converse of that commandment which is: "Only parents who are honorable can be truly honored."

Marriage is a commitment. So often young people want to sentimentalize the service, make it pretty and pleasant and folksy without coming to grips with the fact that marriage is a solemn covenant entered into by two individuals in the presence of God. This becomes a promise of hard work, duty, fidelity, responsibility and obligation. These are not always fun words or fun actions. But any lasting monument is built only by mutually creative action filled with laughter and tears, joys and sorrows—moving from strength to strength. These are obligations, beyond self, that never end.

Church membership is a commitment. The basic vow of church membership is the response to a question of faith: "Do you believe in Jesus Christ as your Lord and Savior?" "Yes," answers the confirmand, with a mental and emotional assertion of something that is felt within. Then, in order to give some kind of minimal standards of measurement to the subjective question, another response is requested. "Will you attend church regularly and support the church to the best of your ability?" This is the command of Christ: "go to the vineyard." And when one says yes to that obligation our Lord expects him to keep his word. The action indicates the sincerity of the promise: "I go, sir." Presenting our sacrificial tithes and offerings each Sunday morning is not a routine event by which we regularly pay the rent. This is one of the high moments of worship. Here we express anew our love and devotion. In this loving act we reaffirm our faith. As a company of God's people we give visible witness to deeply held convictions. As individual Christians we renew our commitment to Jesus Christ as Lord and Savior by doing as well as by saying. And we reach out to the world in Christ's name, as commanded.

Often, we demand as a mark of integrity that a person practice what he preaches. On Calvary our Lord did just that. He went to Jerusalem knowing he had to go, even though the days of his short years were numbered. He cleansed the Temple, knowing that he was challenging the religious authorities. He refused to barter with Pilate, knowing that he was defying the imperial power of Caesar. He left Gethsemane, knowing that he was about to die. This was the price love would have to pay. This was his offering. God had sent him to the vineyard. He had committed himself and there was no turning back. He was as good as his word. In John's gospel he says, "My meat is to do the will of him that sent me, and to finish the work" (John 4:34b—KJV).

God had commissioned him and God was depending on him. Yet, Christ acted out of free will. He had made a decision. He constantly withstood the temptation to default. He was torn between the loyalty of promise and what he wanted to do when he prayed, "Not my will, but thine be done." When the moment came that God would give his son for the redemption of the world he asked him to go to the vineyard and Christ answered, " 'I go, sir': and he went." He kept his word. And through him, God keeps his promise of redemption to all mankind.

The cross, redemption, salvation and eternal life are all kept promises on our behalf: commitments fulfilled. God our Father addresses us as his children and says, "Go to the vineyard." We

127

are his true heirs when we say, "I go, sir," and keep the pledge. Our sonship is the test of our deeds—the daily, common, routine expressions and those actions of living out the faith we profess. The Apostle John writes, "And hereby we do know that we know him, if we keep his commandments. He that saith, I know him, and keepeth not his commandments is a liar, and the truth is not in him. But whoso keepeth his word, in him verily is the love of God perfected: hereby know we that we are in him. He that saith he abideth in him ought himself also so to walk, even as he walked" (I John 2:3-6—KJV).

Rufus Jones tells a delightful story about a blacksmith in a small Maine town. The blacksmith was so extremely short of stature that he was very humble-minded. He fell deeply in love with the tallest and fairest girl in the village, but he did not dare to tell her of his love and for years he kept the secret locked in his heart. One day, however, the girl came into his shop to have something made. He pounded it out for her on his anvil, and she was so warmly appreciative that then and there he proposed to her. She accepted him on the spot, and leaping on his anvil he kissed her heartily. Then he asked her to take a walk with him, which she did. After a suitable time he asked if he might kiss her again, but she refused. "Not here in public," she said. "Well then," he replied, "if there isn't going to be any more kissing, I'm not carrying this anvil any farther. It's heavy."

This is a parable. Life isn't all kissing. It is more often than not carrying anvils. Those things to which we commit ourselves are often costly enterprises. But, when the grapes are harvested, when commitments are being fulfilled, when promises are being kept, when one continues to honor his word, then there is also the joy of celebration. We stand on the anvil of commitment in order to kiss the joy of attainment. And all the while we press on (in commitment) "toward the goal for the prize of the upward call of God in Christ Jesus."

That, in part, is what Loyalty Sunday means. Under the burden (anvil) of our Christian responsibility and accountability, but at the same time as a love expression of our voluntary commitment to Christ as Lord and Savior, we sacrificially pledge and covenant to the glory of God. It means a present and long-range spiritual discipline which comes out of our understanding of God's requirements for the strengthening of his people. For the burden of the word of God is at the same time our only hope and our true salvation. In response to the overwhelming love of God and the magnificent example of Jesus Christ let us commit ourselves anew to sacrificial stewardship. Let us do so with joy and generosity.

· 18 ·

"TWO TO ONE"—THE POSSIBLE DREAM

ONE of the vital signs of a living church is the size of its benevolent heart. There is a direct relationship between spiritual strength and financial stewardship. The giving of gifts can be described in specific figures representing measurable amounts. Set against goals, sums can picture degrees of actual attainment and achievement.

Of much more significance is the subjective factor. Giving is also an expression of faith. It may be an overt act. But it is also a way of externalizing inner convictions. Faith needs to be objective as well as subjective. St. Paul writes in II Corinthians 9:13 (J. B. Phillips translation) ". . . your very giving proves the reality of your faith." Stewardship is not always considered in that light. More often it is thought of in terms of goals, formulas or budgets to be met.

Paul tells us that giving is actually the proof of what we believe or literally a profession of faith. Faith needs to be kept and given away—kept in the heart and expressed in "an overflowing tide of thanksgiving to God." The corporate faith of a congregation is demonstrated by what a church does with its money even as an individual's giving is an indication of the reality of his faith. By the same token, an individual is strengthened in his convictions (and corresponding tangible response) by the attitude, philosophy and example of his particular church. Unfortunately, many churches fail to stimulate the faith-response of a congregation because there is no obvious sacrificial corporate commitment.

The "two to one" concept of corporate stewardship has had a profound influence on the life of our particular congregation (one dollar given to general mission for every two dollars spent on local mission). But in order for it to work a congregation must work at it. It doesn't just happen.

Like tithing, it is a matter of faith, conviction, discipline, priority and practice. Like tithing, it has its configurations of costliness. Like tithing, it has its joys and blessings. Like tithing, it can be brought out of the realm of the impossible dream. Like tithing, it can become real for those who want to make it real. Like tithing, it can become an expression of genuine faith. Like tithing, it can work with any size budget (and any size church). Like tithing, it becomes easier and yet more exciting as it is practiced. Like tithing, when the commitment is there, the resources are always available. Like tithing, significant spiritual growth takes place along with the giving process.

About twelve years ago the officers of our congregation began to draw up a ten-year plan for renewal and development. Considerable time, thought and study were given to such items as building improvement for more effective ministry, implementation of staff, community role and involvement, increased evangelism, spiritual development within the congregation and enrichment of our programs. The Interpretation and Stewardship Committee, aware of the local mission costs of such projects, challenged the officers by suggesting that "two to one" giving be included as one of the goals of the ten year plan.

At that point in time the suggestion seemed like an impossible dream, in light of projected and immediate needs. Obviously there was considerable discussion. Benevolence support had been increasing steadily. Nevertheless, as in most churches, local mission needs had priority so that benevolence giving was not keeping pace with local mission expenditures.

The officers had some reservations about anything so daring as "two to one" giving, although they appreciated the principle. Practically, it appeared out of the question. The Interpretation and Stewardship Committee persisted. They reminded the officers that a church urged its members to make sacrificial gifts as part of their spiritual commitment and that they should give the church priority in their charitable concerns. The church then should practice the same principle by making benevolences a sacrificial priority. In its own way, the church needed to practice what it was preaching. It should thoughtfully weigh what it was spending on itself with a proportionate concern for general mission.

"Two to one" giving, as a venture in faith, was incorporated in the ten-year plan. It was carefully and positively interpreted to the congregation. They heard the message, understood the principle and accepted the proportion. Within two years we became a "two to one" congregation and have maintained and exceeded that proportion for the past ten years.

The "two to one" proportion has vitalized the giving of this particular church. The members know and appreciate what it means. They are aware of the significance of the general mission budget and believe in its place of priority. They see it as part of their spiritual commitment and involvement. Their own stewardship has been enriched and enlarged by the example of corporate commitment on the part of their church.

At the same time, officers and staff exercise careful oversight of the local mission budget in order to maintain a sound balance without compromising local program or mission. This is responsible discipline. It means constant scrutiny of congregational spending for self, and giving to others. Self needs in a congregation can become an obsession to the point of obliterating the vast needs beyond. "Two to one" offers a proportionate balance along with a broadened perspective. It serves as a barrier to compromise, rationalization and tokenism. It forces a congregation to be honest with itself and the whole mission of the church. No local congregation contains or represents the whole mission of the

church. "Two to one" giving stimulates stewardship growth by offering a challenging proportion
and perspective.

More realistically, it is a significant venture of
faith. At that point God takes over and the mys-
terious process of his multiplication becomes
operative. Not only are all needs met, but the
"baskets full of leftovers" become a serendipity
of his grace.

Index of Illustrative Material

Bibliography

Anderson, Michael D. *A Present Witness* (Bible Study and comments on Stewardship and Mission). Wilton, Ct.: Morehouse-Barlow Co. 1975.

Balcomb, Raymond E. *Stir What You've Got and Other Stewardship Studies.* Nashville, Tenn.: Abingdon Press. 1968.

Bayne, Raymond. *Before The Offering: Mini Messages on Giving.* Grand Rapids, Mich.: Baker Book House. 1971.

Bratgard, Helge. *God's Stewards* (A Theological Study of the Principles and Practices of Stewardship). Minneapolis, Minn.: Augsburg Publishing House. 1963.

Briggs, Edwin. *Theological Perspectives on Stewardship.* Nashville, Tenn.: General Board of the Laity, Division of Stewardship and Finance, The United Methodist Church. 1969.

Carlson, Martin E. *Why People Give.* Wilton, Ct.: Morehouse-Barlow Co. 1973.

Clark, Henry B. *Escape from the Money Trap.* Valley Forge, Pa.: Judson Press. 1973.

Crawford, John R. *A Christian and His Money.* Nashville, Tenn.: Abingdon Press. 1967.

Crockett, W. David. *Promotion and Publicity for Churches.* Wilton, Ct.: Morehouse-Barlow Co. 1973.

_____. *Sound Financial Stewardship.* Wilton, Ct.: Morehouse-Barlow Co. 1973.

Crowe, Charles M. *Stewardship Sermons.* Nashville, Tenn.: Abingdon Press. 1960.

Davenport, Arthur, ed. *The Ten Best Stewardship Sermons.* Oklahoma City, Okla.: Arthur Davenport Associates, Inc. 1963.

Dietze, Charles. *God's Trustees.* St. Louis, Mo.: Bethany Press. 1976.

Ditzen, Lowell R. *The Minister's Desk Book.* West Nyack, N. Y.: Parker Publishing Co., Inc. 1968.

137

Dollar, Truman. *How To Carry Out God's Stewardship Plan*. New York, N. Y.: Thomas Nelson. 1974.

Eller, Vernard. *The Simple Life*. Grand Rapids, Mich.: Eerdmans. 1973.

Ferenback, Campbell. *Preaching Stewardship*. Edinburgh: St. Andrews Press. 1967.

Fisher, Wallace E. *A New Climate For Stewardship*. Nashville, Tenn.: Abingdon Press. 1976.

Haldeman, I. M. *The Tabernacle, Priesthood and Offerings*. Old Tappan, N. J.: Fleming H. Revell Co. 1976.

Harrell, W. C. *Stewardship and the Tithe*. Nashville, Tenn.: Abingdon Press. 1970.

Harrison, George W. *Fund Raising*. Englewood Cliffs, N. J.: Prentice-Hall, Inc. 1964.

Hengel, Martin. *Property and Riches in the Early Church*. Philadelphia, Pa.: Fortress Press. 1970.

Hess, Bartlett L. and Margaret Johnston Hess. *How to Have a Giving Church*. Nashville, Tenn.: Abingdon Press. 1974.

Hoekendyk, J. J. *The Church Inside Out*. Philadelphia, Pa.: Westminster Press. 1966.

Holck, Manfred. *Annual Church Budgeting*. Minneapolis, Minn.: Augsburg Publishing House. 1977.

_____. *Church Cash Management*. Minneapolis, Minn.: Augsburg Publishing House. 1978.

_____. *Money and Your Church*. New Canaan, Conn.: Keats Publishing, Inc. 1974.

Hollis, Allen. *The Bible and Money*. New York, N. Y.: Hawthorn Books. 1976.

Holt, David R. *Handbook of Church Finance*. New York, N. Y.: Macmillan, Inc. 1960.

Hudnut, Robert K. *The Sleeping Giant*. New York, N. Y.: Harper and Row. 1971.

Johnson, Douglas W. and Cornell, George W. *Punctured Preconceptions—What North American Christians Think About the Church*. New York, N. Y.: Friendship Press. 1972.

Kantonen, T. A. *A Theology For Christian Stewardship*. Philadelphia, Pa.: Muhlenberg Press. 1956.

Kauffman, Milo. *Stewards of God*. Scottdale, Pa.: Herald Press. 1975.

King, Julius, ed. *Successful Fund Raising Sermons*. New York, N. Y.: Funk and Wagnalls Co. 1953.

Bibliography

Knudson, Raymond B. *New Models For Creative Giving.* New York, N. Y.: Association Press. 1976.

———. *New Models for Financing the Local Church.* New York, N. Y.: Association Press. 1974.

Kuntz, Kenneth. *Wooden Chalices* (New Ideas for Stewardship). St. Louis, Mo.: The Bethany Press. 1963.

Leach, William H. *Handbook of Church Management.* Englewood Cliffs, N. J.: Prentice-Hall, Inc. 1958.

MacNaughton, John H. *Stewardship: Method and Myth.* New York, N. Y.: Seabury Press. 1975.

McKay, Arthur R. *Servants and Stewards.* Philadelphia, Pa.: The Geneva Press. 1963.

McMullen, John S. *Stewardship Unlimited.* Richmond, Va.: John Knox Press. 1964.

Murphy, Nordan C. *Commitment Plan Handbook.* Published cooperatively by 14 denominations. Available: Cokesbury Book Stores.

O'Connor, Elizabeth. *Eighth Day of Creation: Gifts and Creativity.* Waco, Texas.: Word Books. 1972.

Page, Harry R. *Church Budget Development.* Englewood Cliffs, N. J.: Prentice-Hall, Inc. 1964.

Pappenleim, Eugene. *Stewardship Without Failure.* Milwaukee, Wis.: Agape Press. 1975.

Piper, Otto A. *The Christian Meaning of Money.* Englewood Cliffs, N. J.: Prentice-Hall, Inc. 1965.

Powell, Luther P. *Money and the Church.* New York, N. Y.: Association Press. 1962.

Rieke, Thomas C. and John C. Espie. *Opportunities in Stewardship.* Nashville, Tenn.: Discipleship Resources, Tidings. 1975.

Rolston, Holmes. *Stewardship in the New Testament Church.* Richmond, Va.: 1959.

Salstrand, George A. E. *The Story of Stewardship in America.* Grand Rapids, Mich.: Baker Book House 1956.

Schaller, Lyle E. *Hey, That's Our Church!* Nashville, Tenn.: Abingdon Press. 1975.

———. *Parish Planning.* Nashville, Tenn.: Abingdon Press. 1974.

Select Stewardship Sermons. Lima, Ohio.: C.S.S. Publishing Co. 1973.

Shedd, Charlie W. *How to Develop a Tithing Church.* Nashville, Tenn.: Abingdon Press. 1961.

Taylor, John V. *Enough is Enough*. Minneapolis, Minn.: Augsburg Publishing House. 1977.

Thompson, T. K. *Stewardship in Contemporary Life*. New York, N. Y.: Association Press. 1965.

Thompson, T. K., ed. *Stewardship in Contemporary Theology*. New York, N. Y.: Association Press. 1960.

Towards a Christian Attitude to Money: Papers and Findings from an Ecumenical Consultation. Geneva: World Council of Churches. 1966.

Turnbull, Ralph G. *Baker's Dictionary of Practical Theology*. Grand Rapids, Mich.: Baker Book House. 1972.

Twenty Stewardship Sermons. Minneapolis, Minn.: Augsburg Publishing House. 1960.

Ward, Hiley H. *Creative Giving*. New York, N. Y.: The Macmillan Co. 1958.

Werning, Waldo J. *The Stewardship Call*. St. Louis, Mo.: Concordia Publishing House. 1965.

Young, Samuel. *Giving and Living: Foundations for Christian Stewardship*. Kansas City, Mo.: Beacon Hill Press. 1974.

Other Sources of Stewardship Material

Arthur Davenport Associates, Inc.
Stewardship Promotional Materials for the ·Local
Church: P. O. Box 18545, Oklahoma City, Okla. 73118.
Christian Stewardship Development, Inc.
Stewardship Campaign Materials: P. O. Box 35623,
Tulsa, Okla. 74135.
Church and Clergy Finance
Bi-weekly financial newsletter for ministers edited by
Manfred Holck: Ministers' Life Resources, Minneapolis,
Minn.
Church Development, Inc.
Seminars and Illustrative Materials: 3868 Constitution
Ave., Colorado Springs, Colo. 80909.
Church Fund Raising Institute
Information on Fund Raising: 222 N. Wells St., Number
1411, Chicago, Ill. 60602.
Church Management—The Clergy Journal, edited by
Manfred Holck:
Church Management, Inc., 4119 Terrace Lane, Hopkins,
Minn. 55343.
Denominational Headquarters
Interpretation and Stewardship materials for local con-
gregations.
Family Films
Dynamic Giving: Multi-Media Kit of Christian Steward-
ship Resources, Panorama City, Cal. 91402.
Journal of STEWARDSHIP, published annually by the
Commission on Stewardship of the National Council of
Churches, 475 Riverside Dr., New York, N. Y. 10027.
Kairos
Stewardship Aids for the Local Church: Box 24056,
Minneapolis, Minn. 55424.

141

THE ART OF CHURCH CANVASS

Lay Publications
The Faith-Action Evangelistic Stewardship Commitment Plan: Box 19714—Dept. C J, Milwaukee, Wis. 53219.
Neibauer Press
Stewardship, Mission and Communication Materials for the Local Church: 20 Industrial Dr., Ivyland, Pa. 18974.
Parish Publications
Stewardship Publications for the Local Church: 32401 Industrial Drive, Madison Heights, Mich. 48071.
S.A.L.T. (Stewardship Aids Leadership Training)
Bi-monthly Stewardship Letter for the Local Church. Published by Salt Publishing Co., a division of the Louis Neibauer Co., 20 Industrial Dr., Ivyland, Pa. 18974.
Scriptographic Books
Channing L. Bete Co., Inc., Greenfield, Mass.
Your Church, edited by Richard Crist (six times annually): The Religious Publishing Co., 198 Allendale Rd., King of Prussia, Pa. 19406.

142